The best of
LONDON

NICK HANNA

NEW
HOLLAND

GLOBETROTTER™

First edition published in 2005
by New Holland Publishers (UK) Ltd
London • Cape Town • Sydney • Auckland
10 9 8 7 6 5 4 3 2 1

website: www.newhollandpublishers.com

Garfield House, 86 Edgware Road
London W2 2EA
United Kingdom

80 McKenzie Street
Cape Town 8001
South Africa

14 Aquatic Drive
Frenchs Forest, NSW 2086
Australia

218 Lake Road
Northcote, Auckland
New Zealand

Distributed in the USA by
The Globe Pequot Press, Connecticut

Copyright © 2005 in text: Nick Hanna
Copyright © 2005 in maps: Globetrotter
Travel Maps
Copyright © 2005 in photographs:
Individual photographers as credited (right)
Copyright © 2005 New Holland Publishers
(UK) Ltd

ISBN 1 84330 835 5

Publishing Manager (UK): Simon Pooley
Publishing Manager (SA): Thea Grobbelaar
DTP Cartographic Manager: Genené Hart
Editor: Thea Grobbelaar

Designer: Nicole Engeler
Cartographer: Genené Hart
Picture Researcher: Shavonne Johannes
Proofreader: Claudia dos Santos

Reproduction by Resolution (Cape Town) and
Hirt & Carter (Pty) Ltd, Cape Town
Printed and bound by Times Offset (M) Sdn. Bhd.,
Malaysia.

Although every effort has been made to ensure
that this guide is up to date and current at time
of going to print, the Publisher accepts no
responsibility or liability for any loss, injury or
inconvenience incurred by readers or travellers
using this guide.

Front Cover: *Trafalgar Square.*
Title Page: *Westminster by night.*

CONTENTS

MAKE THE MOST OF YOUR GUIDE

Reading these two pages will help you to get the most out of your guide and save you time when using it. Sites discussed in the text are cross-referenced with the cover maps – for example, the reference 'Map C–B3' refers to the Central London Map (Map C), column B, row 3. Use the Map Plan below to quickly locate the map you need.

MAP PLAN

Outside Back Cover   Outside Front Cover

Inside Front Cover   Inside Back Cover

THE BIGGER PICTURE

Key to Map Plan

A – Windsor and Eton
B – Hampton Court
C – Central London
D – London City Centre
E – Greenwich
F – Greater London
G – Excursions
H – London Under-
ground Map

Key to Symbols

⊠ – address

☎ – telephone

℘ – fax

💻 – website

✍ – e-mail address

🕑 – opening times

🚌 – tour

💰 – entry fee

🍴 – restaurants nearby

⊖ – nearest tube station

Map Legend

motorway		motorway	
primary route		main road	**Millbank**
main road		other road	Old Queen St
river	Thames	mall	MILLENNIUM BRIDGE
route number	M1 A406	built-up area	
city	LONDON	post office	⊠
major town	⊙ Oxford	parking area	P
small town	○ Stratford-upon-Avon	police station	●
airport	✈	hospital	⊕
place of interest	● Wembley Stadium	underground station	● Paddington
railway		docklands light railway	● Greenwich
golf course	⌐	one-way street	→
hotel	Ⓗ GORING	library	◫
building of interest	County Hall	place of worship	△ St Bride's
shopping centre	Ⓢ Harrods	tourist information	ⅰ
		park & garden	Green Park

Keep us Current

Travel information is apt to change, which is why we regularly update our guides. We'd be most grateful to receive feedback from you if you've noted something we should include in our updates. If you have any new information, please share it with us by writing to the Publishing Manager, Globetrotter, at the office nearest to you (addresses on the imprint page of this guide). The most significant contribution to each new edition will be rewarded with a free copy of the updated guide.

Above: *Running through the heart of London, the River Thames has always played a crucial role in the city's history.*

LONDON

'When a man is tired of London he is tired of life', wrote Samuel Johnson – a sentiment which is no less true today than it was in the 18th century. It is one of great capitals of the world, the largest city in Europe, and the central focus of politics, art, entertainment, the media, the judiciary and much else in Britain.

The Land
The Thames

London developed at the point nearest the mouth of the Thames, where it was feasible to build bridges and anchor large ships in deep water. The Thames is a tidal river, and extensive areas on either side of its banks are classified as flood plains. In Roman times, areas south of the river were often inundated. Over the centuries the south-east of England has been gradually tilting towards the sea, and London would still be subject to flooding from surge tides were it not for the Thames Barrier.

Climate

London has a temperate climate, but it's almost impossible to generalize about the weather here, since it is highly changeable. **Spring** is generally pleasant, although cold March winds and April showers can occur; **summer** often has sweltering heat followed by thunderstorms and overcast conditions; **autumn** can vary from summer-like days in September to crisp, clear weather in October,

---

River Management
Once the Thames was a dumping ground for everything from sewage to the effluents of Victorian factories. A major clean-up campaign has seen fish return to these waters, and there is also a fair amount of bird life, which is at its most prolific towards the vast Thames Estuary and in the superb **Wetland Centre** at Barnes. Managing the Thames is the responsibility of the Port of London Authority (PLA), which controls a 150km (93-mile) section of the river stretching from the Thames Estuary all the way up to Teddington Lock.

with November one of the wettest months; **winter** is a season you should come well prepared for, with cold conditions and rain, hail, sleet or even snow a possibility.

Flora and Fauna

London's parks, squares and public gardens are home to a huge variety of **plant life**. Regent's Park is known for its displays of colourful flower borders. Hyde Park and Kensington Gardens offer a variety of trees, flowers and shrubberies, while Battersea Park features blooming cherry and acacia in the spring. Richmond Park is renowned for its magnificent oak trees, as well as thickets of flowering rhododendrons.

London has a surprising variety of **bird life**. The Serpentine in Hyde Park is frequented by swans, tufted ducks, mallards, great crested grebes, moorhens, coots, and herons. St James's Park is famous for its pelicans. The largest of the royal parks, Richmond, is home to kestrels, nuthatches, great spotted woodpeckers and numerous waterfowl, and also rabbits, squirrels and deer. Foxes are a common sight in the London suburbs.

> **Deer in the Park**
> There are around 600 red and fallow deer in **Richmond Park**, easily seen almost everywhere because they are still enclosed by Charles I's tall walls. They breed prolifically, and hence have to be culled twice yearly. If you want to watch the mating displays of the red deer at their most dramatic, visit during autumn, when the stags battle it out over their harems of hinds, great antlers crashing together as they duel. Don't go near young deer in the spring, as their mothers may then desert them.

Below: *A fallow deer buck in Richmond Park, one of London's wildlife havens.*

History in Brief

In AD43 a **Roman** invasion force landed at Richborough in Kent. Their goal was Camulodunum (Colchester), which became the Roman capital. In AD60 a rebellion by the **Iceni** tribes, under **Queen Boudicca** (Boadicea), led to the sacking of Camulodunum and a massacre of

Below: *Staple Inn in Holborn, one of the few timber-framed buildings to survive the Great Fire.*

the inhabitants of the river crossing at **Londinium**. After the defeat of the Iceni (and Boudicca's suicide) Londinium was rebuilt as the main Roman base in Britain, prospering until the withdrawal of the Romans in the 5th century AD.

By the 14th century London's population had reached around 80,000 people but the **Black Death** (1348) wiped out over a third of them. During the 15th century trade with other countries continued to expand. London became a centre for world commerce, with the opening up of trade routes to the Orient and the discovery of America.

Under **Elizabeth I** England enjoyed considerable prosperity. The Tudor dynasty ended in 1603 with her death.

In 1665, London was hit by an outbreak of the bubonic plague, and the following year another major disaster occurred when the **Great Fire** of 1666 destroyed large areas of the city; it did, however, wipe out the last remnants of the plague, and also led to the rebuilding of several landmarks.

In 1801, when the first official census was taken, London's population stood at around one million inhabitants, making it the most **populous** city in Europe. Over the next century it grew to nearly seven million as the city became increasingly industrialized and developed as the commercial and administrative hub of the British Empire.

During the reign of **Queen Victoria**, roads, railways and houses continued to be built across the capital, and docks were developed on the banks of the Thames. The city's first railway line (from London Bridge to Greenwich) was

opened in 1836, and the first underground line (between Paddington and Farringdon Road) was built in 1863.

At the outbreak of **World War I** in August 1914 the crowds in London cheered, but it became apparent that

it was not going to be 'all over by Christmas'. The first bombs fell on Stoke Newington in May 1915, but casualties in the capital were slight compared to those in Belgium and northern France.

At the outbreak of **World War II** in 1939 trench shelters were dug in London's parks, over 600,000 women and children were evacuated to the countryside, and the strict enforcement of night-time blackouts led to a huge increase in road accidents. But the bombs didn't arrive for another year, with the start of the Blitz in September 1940, marked by many deaths and injuries.

Victory in Europe (VE) Day, in 1945, was followed by a general election, where Winston Churchill was defeated by Clement Attlee's Labour Party. The **Welfare State** was created and the government embarked on wholesale nationalization of industries. But in London the most pressing problem was a shortage of houses: prefabricated buildings were erected all over the city and massive high-rise housing estates were built on derelict bomb sites. In an attempt to relieve the austerity of day-to-day life, the **Festival of Britain** was staged in 1951 on the south bank of the Thames; the site eventually became the South Bank Centre.

Above: *The Map Room, one of the Cabinet War Rooms where Churchill and his Cabinet held meetings during World War II.*

The Blitz

During the Blitz, the Luftwaffe bombed the capital for 57 consecutive nights, and Londoners sought shelter in the underground stations or purpose-built shelters in their gardens. Firemen and thousands of volunteers fought bravely to contain the fires and rescue those buried in the rubble of their houses. The worst night came on 29 December 1940, when thousands of incendiary bombs threatened to set the capital alight. By the end of the Blitz, in May 1941, over a third of the City and the East End lay in ruins; over 30,000 people had died, with 50,000 injured and 130,000 houses destroyed.

Above: *The Millennium Dome is now a sports and entertainment venue.*
Opposite: *Inside the House of Lords.*

Social Unrest

During the Thatcher years social polarities in the capital increased, with stark contrasts between the rise in long-term unemployment and the conspicuous consumption enjoyed by the professional classes ('yuppies'). Riots erupted in Brixton in 1981 and Tottenham in 1985, and homelessness in the capital reached levels not witnessed since Victorian times. An area around the South Bank became known as 'Cardboard City' due to the many vagrants living in cardboard shelters on the pavements. This has now been cleared out by the area's redevelopment, but 'dossers' in London doorways remain a common sight.

During the 1950s the population of the capital fell, although there was also a large influx of immigrants from the former colonies and the Caribbean. The 'Swinging Sixties' heralded a new era of liberation, and 'groovy' London became the music and fashion capital of the world.

The 1970s seemed drab by comparison, with economic austerity leading to the three-day week in 1974 and the downfall of the Conservative government. Britain became part of the EEC, and the IRA started a bombing campaign on the mainland. In the late 1970s **Margaret Thatcher** came into power and began a process of privatization and cuts in public services which was to leave few areas untouched.

The crash of the money markets in 1987 led to a deepening recession. In 1990, riots in Trafalgar Square against the poll tax signalled the beginning of the end for Margaret Thatcher, who was replaced as leader of the Conservative Party by **John Major**. The seven years of growing dissatisfaction with Conservative rule that followed led to **Tony Blair** and his New Labour Party sweeping into power in May 1997.

Some grandiose new structures mark London's transition into the 21st century. Among them are the Millennium Dome in Greenwich, the conversion of Bankside Power Station into Tate Modern, and the innovative pedestrian Millennium Bridge linking Bankside with the city.

Government and Economy

The UK is a constitutional monarchy, and the Queen has the power to veto legislation. The Prime Minister and his Cabinet of key ministers place legislation before Parliament for ratification. Sitting in the Palace of Westminster, Parliament consists of 659 elected Members of the House of Commons and the unelected House of Lords.

Local Government

In 1965, the London County Council was replaced by the Greater London Council (GLC), which was responsible for a wide range of services and strategic planning. The GLC found itself at odds with central Government and was abolished in 1986. But in 1998 a referendum decided that Greater London should have an elected mayor and its own assembly, responsible for transport, fire, police and other services.

Economy

London continues to dominate in the political and financial arenas and leads the UK in many other areas including the arts, culture, fashion, publishing, retailing, the media and much else besides. Tourism is an important component of the economy.

London is the longest established of the world's primary financial centres, and is the largest centre for foreign exchange trading. Most of Europe's top law firms have offices in the city, as do around a quarter of Europe's top 100 media companies.

Governing London

The first step towards creating a governing body – the mark of a true city – was the establishment of the Metropolitan Board of Works in 1855. In 1888, the LCC (London County Council) became the first elected ruling body and was responsible for building County Hall, its headquarters. London now has 31 boroughs (plus the Cities of Westminster and London, the latter being London's commercial and financial heartland) and each has its own Lord Mayor, of which the best known is the 'Lord Mayor of London' (actually Lord Mayor of the City of London). The new post of 'Mayor of London' is an administrative job that covers the whole of the capital.

London's Population
12C Beginnings of the capital: 18,000.
14C Beginnings of overseas trade: 50,000.
1348 Black Death takes half the population.
16C Boom times under the Tudors: 200,000.
1664–65 Great Plague kills 70,000–100,000.
1700 London is now Europe's most populous city: 575,000.
1801 First official census: One million.
1900 Victorian expansion: 6–7 million.
1939 Peak interwar population: 8.7 million.
1940–41 30,000 killed in the Blitz.
1950s Immigration from former colonies: 20,000 annual arrivals.
1960s–70s Decline of manufacturing, flight to suburbs: 500,000 leave the capital.
2004 Around 7.5 million.

Below: *The annual Notting Hill Carnival is the largest street festival in Europe.*

The People

London is a **cosmopolitan** city, attracting people from other nations to live and work here. Today you will find not only the Irish, Italians, Bangladeshis, Germans and West Indians, but also Somalis, Moroccans, Kurds, Portuguese and people from every corner of the globe. No less than 33 countries have resident communities of over 10,000 people who were born outside the UK and now live in the capital.

It is estimated that 200 **languages** are spoken in the city, and it is claimed that over 30% of Londoners are descended from first-, second- and third-generation immigrants. Writer HV Morton concluded in the 1940s that 'one of the charms of London is that there are no Londoners'.

Ethnic London

Londoners tend to associate more with the neighbourhoods in which they live than with the city as a whole. Immigrant groups have tended to settle in certain localities for particular reasons: Punjabi Sikhs, for instance, populated Southall in the vicinity of Heathrow because it was near their point of arrival, and the airport offered work. Cypriots gravitated to Camden and Finsbury, where they could use their skills in the clothing trade, while Bengali Muslims moved to the area around Brick Lane in Tower Hamlets for similar reasons. The Chinese moved into the East End – but the introduction of launderettes precipitated a switch from traditional laundry businesses to Chinese restaurants in Soho. The Afro-Caribbean community has traditionally been based in Brixton and Notting Hill.

Architecture

London's best-known **Norman** building is the Tower of London. The English **Renaissance** is best exemplified by the work of **Inigo Jones**, responsible for the Queen's House at Greenwich, the Banqueting House at Westminster, and the piazza in Covent Garden. The other great architect of the era was Sir Christopher Wren: following the Great Fire in 1666, Wren rebuilt St Paul's Cathedral and numerous other landmarks.

In the 18th century the **neoclassical** style was fashionable, when designer **Robert Adam** remodelled mansions like Kenwood House, Osterley Park and Syon House, and **John Nash** laid out Regent Street, linking St James's Palace with Regent's Park.

Prestigious buildings of the **Victorian** era include the British Museum, the Houses of Parliament, the National Gallery, Tower Bridge, the Natural History Museum, the Royal Albert Hall and St Pancras Station. **Edwardian** London gave us the Old Bailey, Whiteleys, Selfridges and Harrods. The city has few buildings from the **Modernist** era.

The **Postwar** period saw the building of the Royal Festival Hall, the Commonwealth Institute, and dozens of concrete tower blocks. Concrete also predominated in the construction of the South Bank Complex and the Barbican Centre complex.

Notable **post-Modernist** structures include Lloyd's of London, the Canary Wharf tower, the London Ark in Hammersmith, Waterloo International Terminal, the new British Library, the Millennium Dome, the Millennium Bridge, the new city hall and Tate Modern. London's latest new building is the Swiss Re Tower, known as the Gherkin.

Above: *Swiss Re Tower, also known as the Gherkin.*

Cockneys

A 'Cockney' in the broadest sense is anyone born and bred in London, although it usually applies only to working class East End residents – traditionally, only those born within the sound of the bells of St Mary-le-Bow in Cheapside are Cockneys. Cockney rhyming slang thrives in street markets and pubs: 'tit for tat' is a hat, 'apples and pears' are the stairs, and so on. Cockney 'Pearly Kings and Queens' put on traditional costumes for the Costermongers Pearly Harvest Festival Service held at the church of St Martin-in-the-Fields (Trafalgar Square) on the first Sunday every October. A 'costermonger' sells fruit and other produce from a market barrow, and so this is essentially a harvest festival.

🟢 *See* Map D–C5   ★ ★ ★

Houses of Parliament
✉ Palace of Westminster, Westminster, London SW1A 0AA
☎ (020) 7219 4272
📠 (020) 7219 5839
🖥 www.parliament.uk
🕐 Debates in the House of Commons 14:30–22:30 Mon, 11:30–18:30 Tue, Wed, Thu.
⊖ Westminster
♿ Admission is free.
🚌 Guided tours for groups of up to 16 may be arranged.
🍴 Cafés and restaurants in nearby Smith Square.

Jewel Tower
🕐 daily 10:00–17:00 Apr–Oct; 10:00–16:00 Nov–Mar. Last admission 30 min prior to closing.

Opposite: *Westminster Abbey contains the tombs of many medieval monarchs.*
Below: *The Houses of Parliament and Big Ben are best viewed from the south bank of the Thames.*

BIG BEN AND THE HOUSES OF PARLIAMENT

The 'Mother of all Parliaments' is one of London's best-known sights, a grandiose Victorian edifice on the north bank of the Thames, the site of parliamentary meetings since 1265. The 266m (872ft) riverside façade is best appreciated from Westminster Bridge, or the south bank of the Thames, with the imposing Victoria Tower to the west and the clock-tower, containing the bell known as **Big Ben**, to the east.

The House is divided into upper and lower houses, the **House of Commons** and the **House of Lords**. A wartime bomb destroyed the original Commons debating chamber, and reconstruction was completed in 1950. On the other side of the Central Lobby is the House of Lords, a more splendid chamber where debates are usually less acrimonious.

Facing Parliament Square on the north side of the House is **Westminster Hall**, the only surviving relic of the original palace. Across the road from the Houses of Parliament is the 14th-century **Jewel Tower**, which now houses an exhibition on parliament's history.

See Map D–C5 ★★★

WESTMINSTER ABBEY

Westminster Abbey presents a rich pageant of English history and has been the setting for almost every Coronation since 1066. Founded by Edward the Confessor and built on the site of a monastery in the 11th century, the present church mostly dates from the 13th century and its 30m (98ft) nave is the loftiest in the country.

The Abbey is not only the burial place of most monarchs from Henry III (died 1272) through to George II (died 1760), it also commemorates political and artistic idols throughout the history of Britain.

As you enter through the north door, for instance, you will find yourself in **Statesman's Aisle**, where large marble figures represent great politicians such as Gladstone, Disraeli and Robert Peel (founder of the Metropolitan Police, who were originally called 'Bobby's boys' and later just 'bobbies'). In the south transept, **Poet's Corner** has memorials to Chaucer, Shakespeare, Dickens, Byron, Tennyson, Rudyard Kipling, and Thomas Hardy, among others. Many more famous names can be found in **Musician's Aisle** and **Scientist's Corner**.

Other highlights are the **Coronation Chair**, used for the crowning of every monarch since the late 13th century; the **Henry VII Chapel**, which has spectacular vaulting on its ceiling; and the octagonal **Chapter House**, which contains a very fine medieval tiled floor.

Westminster Abbey
✉ Parliament Square, London SW1P 3PA
☎ (020) 7222 5152
📠 (020) 7233 2072
✆ info@ westminster-abbey.org
🖳 www. westminster-abbey.org
⊖ Westminster or St James's Park.
🕘 Mon, Tue, Thu, Fri 09:30–16:45, Wed 09:30–18:00, Sat 09:30–14:45. Last entry 1hr before closing).
♿ There is an admission fee.
🚌 Group tours may be booked ahead:
✆ abbey@ tourguides.co.uk
☎ (020) 7495 5504
📠 (020) 7495 5323 .
🍽 The Coffee Club, in the Cloisters.

TRAFALGAR SQUARE AND THE NATIONAL GALLERY

Named after Nelson's famous naval victory over the French in 1805, Trafalgar Square has as its focal point the 52m (170ft) **Nelson's Column**. On the western side of the square is the neoclassical **Canada House**, echoed on the east side by **South Africa House**. The best view over the square is from the main entrance to the National Gallery, looking down past Nelson's Column and along the length of Whitehall to Big Ben. In the northeast corner of the square is **St Martin-in-the-Fields** (see page 34).

Housing one of the world's greatest permanent art collections, the **National Gallery** contains over 2000 paintings, including famous works of the Old Masters. The collection was begun as late as 1824 with only a few pieces, but today the scope – spanning Western Art from 1250 to around 1900 – is so enormous that it is impossible to absorb it all in one go, so use the (free) floor plan to find your favourite eras.

Around the corner, the **National Portrait Gallery** houses 10,000 portraits (including paintings, drawings, sculptures and photographs) of famous people from the Middle Ages to the present day. The gallery has what is believed to be the only oil portrait of William Shakespeare done from life.

National Gallery
✉ Trafalgar Square, London WC2N 5DN
☎ (020) 7747 2885
📠 (020) 7747 2423
🖥 www.nationalgallery.org.uk
⊖ Charing Cross, Embankment, Leicester Square, Piccadilly Circus
🕐 daily 10:00–18:00, Wed 10:00–21:00; closed: 1 Jan, Good Friday, and 24–26 Dec.
🚌 Tours daily at 11:30 and 14:30
👛 Admission is free.

National Portrait Gallery
✉ St Martin's Place, London WC2H 0HE
☎ (020) 7306 0055
🖥 www.npg.org.uk
⊖ As for National Gallery (see above)
🕐 Sat–Wed 10:00–18:00, Thu, Fri 10:00–21:00. Closed 1 Jan, Good Friday, 24–26 Dec
👛 Free, except some special exhibitions.
🍴 Café in basement, or top-floor Portrait Restaurant; reservations
☎ (020) 7312 2490

☆ See Map D–F2	★ ★ ★

ST PAUL'S CATHEDRAL

St Paul's presents a magnificent **façade**, with its two baroque **towers** capped by a 111m (364ft) dome (second in size only to St Peter's in Rome). Christopher Wren's airy design is immediately apparent on entering, with the impressive **dome** featuring a series of trompe l'œil frescos on the life of St Paul. In the north aisle of the **nave** is a bronze and marble monument to the Duke of Wellington. In the North Transept is Holman Hunt's *The Light of the World*.

The enormous **crypt** is reached via the South Transept, and contains some 350 memorials and over 100 tombs. Recent additions include a memorial to British troops who died in the Falklands, but pride of place goes to the tombs of Wellington and Nelson. Artists (such as Turner and Reynolds) are buried here, as are scientist Alexander Fleming, and Wren himself, whose epitaph reads: 'reader, if you seek his monument, look around you'. The first of the **galleries** under the dome is the Whispering Gallery; the second is the Stone Gallery, and the third is the Golden Gallery (627 steps up) with fabulous views over the city.

South of St Paul's, the innovative **Millennium Bridge** provides great views of the Thames and is also a direct pedestrian link to the **Tate Modern** (*see* page 18).

> **St Paul's Cathedral**
> ✉ Ludgate Hill, London EC4
> ☎ (020) 7236 4128
> ⌨ chapter@ stpaulscathedral.org.uk
> 🖥 www.stpauls.co.uk
> ⊖ St Paul's is a 5-min walk away.
> ⏱ Mon–Sat from 08:30, last entry 16:00. Closed to visitors during special services.
> 🚌 Guided tours 11:00, 11:30, 13:30, 14:00.
> 👶 Concessions under 16s, free under 6s.
> 🍴 Sandwich bars and pubs in Ludgate Hill.

Opposite: *National Gallery and St Martin-in-the-Fields, Trafalgar Square.*
Below: *The dome of St Paul's Cathedral is a London landmark.*

Tate Modern
✉ Bankside, London
SE1 9TG
☎ (020) 7887 8000
🖥 www.tate.org.uk/
modern
⊖ Southwark and
Blackfriars are both less
than a 10-min walk.
🕓 Sun–Thu 10:00–
17:15, Fri and Sat
10:00–21:15
💰 Admission is free,
but donations are wel-
comed to support the
gallery's work.
🍴 There is a café on
Level 2, a restaurant
on Level 7, and an
espresso bar on Level 4.

| ☆ See Map D–F3 | ★ ★ ★ |

TATE MODERN AND MILLENNIUM BRIDGE

What was once an ugly power station is now **Tate Modern**, a stunning architectural mix of new and old, with stupendous views from the 7th-floor restaurant. Much of the Tate's enormous collection had been lan-guishing unseen for decades, due to lack of space. Now, at last, hundreds of paint-ings and sculptures are once again on view. Arranged by subject, rather than style or chronology, there are four themed gal-leries which enable viewers to appreciate the changing styles of the 20th century. Long-established favourites (such as Monet's *Water Lilies* and Rodin's *The Kiss*) mingle with controversial works that many people consider to be totally devoid of artistic merit.

Opposite: *The Tower of London housed prisoners from medieval times.*
Below: *Millennium Bridge, a pedestrian crossing over the River Thames.*

Since Tower Bridge (built in 1894), cen-tral London had had no new Thames bridge and it was felt that a pedestrian crossing linking Bankside with the City of London would be a way to celebrate the new century, so the innovative **Millennium Bridge** was opened in May 2000. The crowd that thronged onto it caused it to sway, frightening many of the people and raising doubts (probably un-founded) about its safety. It closed after only a few days but has now reopened (minus the sway) and provides wonderful views up and down the Thames.

See Map C–H4 | ★ ★ ★

TOWER OF LONDON AND TOWER BRIDGE

Dating from Norman times, the **Tower of London** has over the last 900 years been a palace, a prison, an execution site, an armoury, and is today a repository for the Crown Jewels. The Yeoman Warders (Beefeaters) conduct frequent (free) tours which are both informative and amusing, so highly recommended.

The White Tower has displays of armour, and torture instruments, and on the first floor is the beautiful 11th-century St John's Chapel, the oldest church in London.

Behind the Traitor's Gate is the Bloody Tower, and on its west side is the Queen's House, now the home of the Tower's Governor and closed to the public. Nearby is Tower Green, the site of several executions.

On the northern side of the compound, the Crown Jewels are on display in the Waterloo Barracks. These include the Crown of State, the Koh-i-Noor diamond, sceptres, orbs and other regal paraphernalia.

Tower Bridge was first opened to traffic on 30 June 1894. It was designed so that tall sailing ships could reach the Port of London – ships still have precedence over road traffic, although nowadays the bridge is raised fewer than 1000 times a year.

The Tower Bridge Exhibition provides a lift up the north tower so that you can cross the Thames by the top walkway – with terrific views – to descend the south tower, from where you can visit the Engine Room. There are informative videos en route.

<u>Tower of London</u>
⊠ Tower Hill, London EC3N 4AB
☎ 0870 756 6060
▣ www.hrp.org.uk
⊖ Tower Hill
🕓 Mar–Oct: Tue–Sat 09:00–18:00, Sun–Mon 10:00–18:00 (last admission 17:00); Nov–Feb: Tue–Sat 09:00–17:00, Sun–Mon 10:00–17:00 (last admission 16:00).
🜲 Under 5s free
🍽 New Armouries restaurant, within Tower walls.

<u>Tower Bridge Exhibition</u>
⊠ Tower Bridge, London SE1 2UP
☎ (020) 7403 3761
📠 (020) 7357 7935
▣ enquiries@ towerbridge.org.uk
▣ www. towerbridge.org.uk
⊖ Tower Hill or London Bridge
🕓 10:00–17:30 in summer, 09:30–17:00 in winter.
🜲 There is an admission fee, but children under 5 are free.

See Map D–C1 ★★★

BRITISH MUSEUM

The British Museum never fails to astound one but, given its size, plan for more than one visit. The extraordinary collections span from prehistoric times to the present day.

Founded in the late 18th century, the museum has some seven and a half million exhibits in 88 galleries, requiring a walk of several miles to cover them all. It is one of the country's biggest tourist attractions – and entry is free.

The museum's great strengths are its amazing collections of treasures and artworks from ancient Egypt, Greece and Rome, as well as Asia and the Far East, in addition to superb treasures from Roman and Anglo-Saxon Britain.

It's impossible to digest it all at once, and you might like to visit several times, or opt for one of the audio or guided tours which cover many of the highlights.

Treasures include the **Rosetta Stone** (dating from 196BC, it provided the key to the decipherment of ancient Egyptian texts); **mummies** of the Pharaohs in the Egyptian Galleries; the **human-headed lions and bulls** of ancient Assyria; the **Elgin Marbles** and other Greek masterpieces; the **Portland Vase** with its exquisitely carved blue and white glass; the **Lindow Man** (sacrificed during a Druidic ceremony, his well-preserved body was found in peat in 1984), and the **Sutton Hoo** Anglo-Saxon treasures.

Above: *The British Museum's collection was largely built up during the days of the Empire.*
Opposite: *Covent Garden is one of the city's most fashionable districts.*

British Museum
✉ Great Russell Street, London WC1B 3DG
☎ (020) 7323 8299
📠 (020) 7323 8616
🖥 www. thebritishmuseum.ac.uk
⊖ Holborn, Tottenham Court Road, Russell Square, Goodge
🕐 Sat–Wed 10:00–17:30, Thu and Fri 10:00–20:30
🔴 Admission free except for temporary exhibitions; children 16 and under free; a fee is payable for tours.
🚌 Guided and audio tours available.
🍴 Great Court restaurant, Gallery café or Court café.

🌐 *See Map D–D3*   ★ ★ ★

COVENT GARDEN

At the core of Covent Garden is the **piazza**, London's oldest planned square, which was designed by Inigo Jones in the 1630s. It was a very desirable residential area until market traders started moving in, and, later, insalubrious coffee houses, gambling dens and brothels sprang up around the piazza. The **central market hall**, built in the 1830s (the glass roof was added later), continued to be the country's most important wholesale fruit and vegetable market until it was relocated to Vauxhall in 1974. Today the market hall, piazza and surrounding streets (particularly in the converted warehouses to the north) are crammed with speciality shops, restaurants, pubs and much more.

On the west side of the piazza is **St Paul's Church** – known as the 'Actors' Church' due to its proximity to theatreland – which has numerous memorials to famous actors and actresses. Appropriately enough, the space in front of the church is now the main venue for Covent Garden's lively street entertainers, with an almost non-stop parade of jugglers, mime artists, musicians and other buskers throughout the day and night.

Facing Bow Street on the east side of the piazza is the **Royal Opera House** (*see page 72*).

London's First Police Force

The licentiousness of **Covent Garden** in the 18th century, with its thinly disguised brothels and bawdy houses, led to the formation of the nation's first police force. A magistrate's court had been established in Bow Street in 1748 and two resident magistrates, Henry Fielding (author of *Tom Jones*) and his brother John, set up a force of six plain-clothes policemen, the **Bow Street Runners**. Though they had some success in cleaning up prostitution, lawlessness still ruled: in 1770, the Lord Chancellor, Prime Minister and Prince of Wales were all robbed in broad daylight. Mounted patrols operated from Bow Street from 1805, but only in 1829 was a unified force, the Metropolitan Police, created.

London Eye
✉ Jubilee Gardens, South Bank, London SE1 1GZ
☎ 0870 500 0600
☎ 0870 400 3005 (groups of 10 or more)
🖥 www.british-airways. com/londoneye
⊖ Westminster, Waterloo
🕙 daily May–Sep: Mon–Thu 09:30–20:00, Fri–Sun 09:30–21:00; Jun: Mon–Thu 09:30–21:00, Fri–Sun 09:30–22:00; Jul–Aug 09:30–22:00; Oct–Apr: 09:30–20:00.

London Aquarium
✉ County Hall, South Bank, London SE1 7PB
☎ (020) 7967 8000
📠 (020) 7967 8029
🖥 www. londonaquarium.co.uk
⊖ Westminster, Waterloo
🕙 daily 10:00–18:00
💰 Entrance charge.
🍴 Cafés and food stalls in Waterloo Gardens.

Saatchi Gallery
✉ County Hall, South Bank, London SE17PB
☎ (020) 7928 8195
🖥 www.saatchi-gallery. co.uk
⊖ Westminster, Waterloo
🕙 Sun–Thu 10:00–20:00, Fri–Sun 10:00–22:00.
💰 Entrance charge.

Opposite: *The V&A charts the history of art and design.*
Right: *The London Eye affords an overview of the capital.*

⭐ See Map D–D4	★ ★ ★

LONDON EYE AND COUNTY HALL

Visible from miles away, the **British Airways London Eye** is London's most popular paid attraction. It soars 135m (450ft) above the Thames, the glass capsules providing unrivalled all-round views. 'Flights' last about 30 minutes. To avoid disappointment, book at least two days in advance, either in person at County Hall, or by phone. Have your credit card number handy – it's a recorded service.

South of the London Eye, in County Hall, the **London Aquarium** is on two levels. It is split into geographical areas and tanks recreate all the watery habitats on earth, from freshwater streams to the ocean depths.

Also inside County Hall is the **Saatchi Gallery**, a new space for one of the most influential collections of the so-called Young British Artists (YBAs) of the 1990s. It houses advertising mogul Charles Saatchi's collection of works by contemporary YBAs such as Damien Hirst, Tracey Emin, Chris Ofili, Sarah Lucas and others. Some of the Britart pieces (Hirst's pickled sharks, or Emin's unmade bed, for instance) are world famous and you'll have seen them in the news before – now's your chance to experience the real thing.

See Map C–B6 ★★

SOUTH KENSINGTON

South Kensington is renowned for its high Victorian architecture and three of the world's best museums.

Housing the world's largest collection of decorative art and design pieces, the huge **Victoria and Albert Museum** usually requires more than just one visit. Founded with proceeds from the Great Exhibition of 1851, it is generally known simply as the V&A. Displays include a comprehensive jewellery collection, Europe's largest dress collection, British artefacts of every type, and the largest exhibition of Indian art outside India.

The **Natural History Museum** houses a massive skeleton of a Diplodocus, signalling one of its major attractions for children, fully exploited in the superb **Dinosaur Gallery**. Other popular displays are **Creepy Crawlies** (with enlarged models of all sorts of insects, spiders and crustaceans) and **Ecology** (where all forms of life are found).

The **Science Museum** extends over seven floors. The original museum covered everything from transport to space travel and chemistry to telecommunications, with masses of interactive displays.

The **Wellcome Wing** is an ultramodern hi-tech extension where most of the exhibits are interactive. The basement **Launch Pad** is aimed at children, while everyone can enjoy finding out about themselves in **Who Am I?**, take a **Virtual Voyages** simulated space ride or visit the **Imax** cinema. Much is free, but allow plenty for things like rides, which are not.

V&A Museum
⊠ Cromwell Road, London SW7 2RL
☎ (020) 7942 2000
📠 (020) 7942 2266
💻 vanda@vam.ac.uk
💻 www.vam.ac.uk
⊖ South Kensington
🕐 Tue–Thu 10:00–17.45, Wed and last Fri of month 10:00–22:00.

Natural History Museum
⊠ Cromwell Road, London SW7 5BD
☎ (020) 7942 5011 or (020) 7942 5000
💻 www.nhm.ac.uk
⊖ South Kensington
🕐 Mon–Sat 10:00–17:50 Sun 11:00–17:50. Last entry 17:30.

Science Museum
⊠ Exhibition Road, London SW7 2DD
☎ 0870 870 4868
📠 (020) 7942 4447
📠 sciencemuseum@nmsi.ac.uk
💻 www.sciencemuseum.org.uk
⊖ South Kensington
🕐 daily 10:00–18:00.

Below: Buckingham Palace, the Queen's London residence.

⭐ *See* Map D–B4 ★★

BUCKINGHAM PALACE

Buckingham Palace
✉ Buckingham Palace, London SW1A 1AA
☎ (020) 7766 7300
📞 (020) 7930 9625
📧 information@ royalcollection.org.uk
🖥 www.royal.gov.uk
⊖ Victoria or Green Park
🕐 daily 1 Aug to 28 Sep 09:30–16:15; queuing time 15–20 mins; opening times subject to change at short notice.
💰 Family tickets are available.
🍽 Cafés and restaurants around Victoria Station.

Queen's Gallery
☎ (020) 7766 7301

Royal Mews
🕐 daily 11:00–15:15 Apr–Oct)

The official London residence of the monarch since Queen Victoria's reign, Buckingham Palace has only been open to the public since 1993, when it was decided to admit visitors to the **State Apartments** to help defray the costs of rebuilding **Windsor Castle** (*see* page 33) after a fire. The Palace is only accessible in August to September when the Queen visits her summer retreat in Balmoral.

The most impressive rooms are the richly decorated **Throne Room**, the **State Dining Room**, **Blue Drawing Room** and **Music Room**. The **Ballroom** is the setting for investitures and entertainment, while the **White Drawing Room** is where the family gathers. In the **Queen's Gallery**, selections from the royal art collection are on view.

Further down Buckingham Palace Road, visit the working stables of the **Royal Mews**, designed by John Nash, who was commissioned by the Prince Regent (later crowned George IV). The main attractions are the magnificent gilded and polished state carriages and coaches, in use since 1831.

See Map C–C4	★ ★

HYDE PARK

London's largest park, Hyde Park was originally a hunting ground for Henry VIII, and was first opened to the public during the reign of James I. At the centre is the **Serpentine**, a long, artificial lake popular for rowing (rowboats can be hired). There is also a **swimming club** at the Serpentine, and members pride themselves on swimming all year, especially at Christmas. On the south side of the lake is the **Serpentine Gallery**.

In Hyde Park's northeastern corner is **Marble Arch**, which was moved here in 1851 from outside Buckingham Palace. Across from Marble Arch is **Speaker's Corner**, which has been a rallying point for political dissent since the 1850s, and is now best known for the soap-box orators who regularly entertain the crowds here (particularly on Sunday mornings).

Park Lane runs down the east side of the park to **Hyde Park Corner**, where **Wellington Arch** (for over a century London's smallest police station) offers exhibits about itself and other monuments. On the northwest side of Hyde Park Corner is **Apsley House**, once upon a time the home of the Duke of Wellington.

Along the south of the park is **Rotten Row**, a fashionable bridlepath where the Household Cavalry exercise every morning from their nearby barracks.

> **The Tyburn Gallows**
> The corner of Hyde Park where the Marble Arch now stands was the site of the infamous Tyburn Gallows until they were demolished in 1825. The gallows (also known as the 'Tyburn Tree') coped with the execution of 20 people at a time, and the frequent hangings drew enormous crowds. The condemned were brought from Newgate Prison by cart, sometimes with the noose already in place, and allowed a free drink at ale houses along the way before being tied to the fatal tree; the cart was then whipped away. At the time, over 150 offences (including such minor misdemeanours as petty theft) warranted a one-way ticket to Tyburn.

Below: *Londoners relaxing by the Serpentine, the artificial lake in Hyde Park.*

Shakespeare's Globe
✉ New Globe Walk,
Bankside, London
SE1 9DT
☎ (020) 7902 1400
📠 (020) 7902 1401
🖥 www.
shakespeares-globe.org
⊖ Monument, Mansion
House, Cannon Street
or London Bridge
🕐 May–Sep (theatre
season) daily 09:00–
12:00; Oct–Apr 10:00–
17:00; times may vary
during the season.
Closed 24–25 Dec
🚌 Groups need to
book in advance to
guarantee entry.
👶 Under 5s free.
🍴 Café, grill restau-
rant and coffee shop
on site.

⭐ See Map D–F3   ★ ★

SHAKESPEARE'S GLOBE

Shakespeare's plays were written for his theatre on the banks of the Thames, known as the 'Wooden O', and it was here that *King Lear*, *Macbeth*, *Hamlet* and *Othello* were first staged. It was closed down by the Puritans in 1642. The current recreation is largely due to American film-maker Sam Wanamaker, who came to London in 1949 expecting to find a Globe Theatre and, disappointed, raised funds to rebuild it.

The Globe Theatre is a faithful recreation of the original structure of the early 1600s – the first thatched building in the capital since the Great Fire of London. In summer, Shakespeare's works are presented as they would have been in his day (apart from the fact that there are now actresses). The techniques are best appreciated if you take the tour before attending a performance. A permanent exhibition, **All the World's a Stage**, covers Bankside, Shakespeare, his theatres, actors and audiences. A tour of the actual theatre is included (or a virtual tour when the theatre is in use).

Opposite: *A snuffbox that once belonged to Frederick the Great, now part of the magnificent Gilbert Collection of Decorative Arts.*
Right: *The Globe Theatre, where Shakespeare's plays are performed today as they were in the 1600s.*

See Map D–D3	★★

SOMERSET HOUSE

Built in 1786, on the site of the palace of the Earls of Somerset, this imposing classical building was the first major building in the country to be designed as offices and is now one of the capital's most important showplaces for art.

One wing of the building (entered from the Strand) now houses the **Courtauld Gallery**, one of the finest collections of paintings in the country, containing superb Impressionist and post-Impressionist works alongside masterpieces from other eras, as well as some sculptures and furniture.

Children enjoy splashing in the 55 jets of water (illuminated at night) that cool the central courtyard. It leads to the wing (with another entrance on Victoria Embankment, the first London thoroughfare to be lit by electricity – in 1879) that now houses the **Gilbert Collection of Decorative Arts**, an awe-inspiring 800-piece collection. There's a spectacular display of large ornamental objects in the main gallery: mostly featuring gold, silver and Italian mosaics, and a side gallery has a wealth of such small items as snuffboxes and miniatures – even a jewel-encrusted Portuguese crown.

The **Hermitage Rooms** recreate the décor of the Winter Palace, in order to provide an atmospheric setting for the changing exhibitions of paintings and applied arts on loan from St Petersburg's Hermitage Museum – of which computer screens provide a virtual tour.

Somerset House
✉ Strand, London WC2R 0RN
☎ (020) 7845 4600
🖳 www.somerset-house.org.uk
⊖ Temple, Covent Garden, Charing Cross, Embankment
🕐 daily 10:00–18:00
🍴 Two restaurants and two cafés on site.

Courtauld Gallery
☎ (020) 7848 2526
🖳 www.courtauld.ac.uk
🕐 10:00–18:00 daily (last admission 17:15).
💰 Free Mon 10:00–14:00 (except public holidays); free students, unwaged, under 18s.

Gilbert Collection of Decorative Arts
☎ (020) 7420 9400
🖳 www.gilbert-collection.org.uk
🕐 10:00–18:00
💰 Entrance charge.

Hermitage Rooms
☎ (020) 7845 4630
🖳 www.hermitagerooms.com
🕐 10:00–18:00
💰 Under 16s free.

Above: *The Royal Observatory has set global time for over three centuries.*

See **Map E**   ★★

GREENWICH

Greenwich has several highlights. Britain's seafaring history (from the 15th century to the Falklands War) is the main theme of the **National Maritime Museum** in Greenwich (see page 39). The historic **Queen's House**, designed by Inigo Jones, now hosts changing exhibitions. Wren's **Royal Naval College** boasts the magnificent Painted Hall, and the elegant Chapel, where concerts and recitals are performed.

The **Royal Observatory** sits on the Greenwich Meridian line, and has an interesting display on time and astronomy, with old telescopes and other instruments. One of the exhibits is the first marine chronometer. There's a fine view over Greenwich Park and Queen Anne's House to Canary Wharf, with the *Cutty Sark*'s rigging visible to the left and the Millennium Dome to the right.

Built on the Clyde in 1869, the *Cutty Sark* was one of the last tea clippers. It still has its original gilded teak fittings, rigging on its three masts, and contains a lot of maritime memorabilia. There are colourful figureheads, and some cabins above contain tableaux of what ship life was like.

Gypsy Moth IV looks tiny alongside the *Cutty Sark*. This 16m (52ft) ketch was the first to be sailed around the world single-handed, by Francis Chichester in 1966–67. On his return, he was knighted with Sir Francis Drake's sword. *Gypsy Moth IV* can't be boarded and is rather weather-beaten.

Greenwich Tourist Information Centre
☎ 0870 608 2000.
🖥 www. greenwich.gov.uk

Royal Observatory
✉ Greenwich Park, London SE10
☎ (020) 8312 6565
📠 (020) 8312 6632
🖥 www.nmm.ac.uk
⊖ DLR Cutty Sark
🕙 10:00–17:00 (last admission 16:30). Closed 24–26 Dec.
💰 Free, except for some special events.
🍴 Cafés, restaurants and pubs in Greenwich town centre.

Cutty Sark
✉ Cutty Sark Gardens, London SE10
☎ (020) 8858 3445
📠 (020) 8853 3589
🖥 www.cuttysark.org.uk
⊖ DLR Cutty Sark
🕙 10:00–17:00. Closed 24–26 Dec.
💰 Entry charge.

See Map B–B2 | ★★

KEW GARDENS

Covering 121ha (300 acres) on the banks of the Thames between Richmond and Kew, the **Royal Botanic Gardens** is a fascinating place to visit. It houses one of the greatest collections of plants and plant material in the world, and is a major research centre. Kew Gardens also boasts four of the largest glasshouses in the world.

Pick up a map at the Visitor Centre before setting off to explore the Gardens. Almost directly opposite is the magnificent **Palm House**, a masterpiece of Victorian engineering in iron and glass. To the east is the **Princess of Wales Conservatory**, Kew's most humid environment, noted for giant water lilies and other tropical plants. West of the Palm House is the elegant **Temperate House**, the largest of Kew's glasshouses with many exotic species, citrus fruits, and the world's largest indoor plant (the Chilean Wine Palm). The **Evolution House**, behind it, traces the development of plant life on earth over the last 3500 million years.

Other highlights include a towering **Pagoda**, the **Marianne North Gallery** (with 832 botanical paintings by this Victorian artist) and **Queen Charlotte's Cottage** (once a royal summer house). The smallest royal residence in the country is the intimate **Kew Palace**, tucked away on the north side of the gardens.

Kew Gardens
- ✉ Kew Green, Richmond, Surrey TW9 3AB
- ☎ (020) 8940 1171
- 📠 (020) 8332 5197
- ✆ info@kew.org
- 🖳 www.rbgkew.org.uk
- ⊖ Kew Gardens
- 🕐 daily from 09:30; closing times 16:00–19:30. Galleries close a little earlier. Glasshouse closes 15:30 (winter), 17:30 (summer). Closed 24–25 Dec, 1 Jan.
- 🛉 Admission free to children under 5.
- 🚌 Mar–Nov one-hour tours daily at 11:00 and 14:00. Limited tours in winter.
- 🍴 There are two restaurants, a coffee shop, and takeaway outlets for snacks and drinks within the park.

Below: *Water lilies in the Princess of Wales Conservatory at Kew Gardens.*

See Map B–A6 ★★

HAMPTON COURT PALACE

Set in 24ha (59 acres) of gardens and park-lands adjoining the Thames, Hampton Court is probably the most dazzling of all the royal palaces in England. Of all the monarchs who have lived here it is most closely associated with Henry VIII, and today the tapestry of court life in Tudor times is vividly brought to life by costumed actors leading tours through this rambling, turreted building. Self-guided audio tours are also available. Don't forget to try the renowned maze.

Entering the **palace** you find yourself in Base Court, which leads to Clock Court and Fountain Court, all of which are surrounded by royal apartments. The Great Hall of **Henry VIII's State Apartments** has an ornate double-hammerbeam roof – Shakespeare's players performed here under Elizabeth I. Other major rooms are the Great Watching Chamber, the Haunted Gallery, and the Royal Chapel. The **Queen's Apartments** are largely 18th century, as are the **Georgian Rooms**. Within the **King's Apartments** (built for William III) is a display of weapons in the King's Guard Chamber. The prodigious food consumption of the Royal Court is vividly brought to life in the impressive **Tudor Kitchens**, which have been restored to show the preparation of meals for a feast day in 1542.

Hampton Court Palace

✉ East Molesey, Surrey KT8 9AU
☎ 0870 752 7777
📠 (020) 8781 5362
🖥 www.hrp.org.uk
⊖ 32 mins by direct train from Waterloo to Hampton Court station. Alternatively, take the tube to Richmond, then the R68 bus from Richmond station to the palace.
🕐 Apr–Oct Mon 10:15–18:00, Tue–Sun 09:30–18:00; Nov–Mar Mon 10:15–16:30, Tue–Sun 09:30–16:30; closed 24–26 Dec and 1 Jan. Gardens open all year round from 07:00 to dusk.
💰 Admission fee, family tickets available.
🍽 Coffee shop, licensed buffet restaurant, picnic areas.

Below: *Riverboats at Hampton Court.*

See Map C–D2 ★

MADAME TUSSAUD'S

This famous waxworks museum attracts millions of visitors and you should expect to queue a long time for tickets. You can avoid the worst queue by purchasing tickets in advance: sources include the tourist buses.

Madame Tussaud's waxworks first came to London in 1802, after its creator fled the French Revolution, escaping the guillotine by moulding death masks of the Revolution's victims. Her last work, a self-portrait, is on display in the museum today.

World Stage covers religious leaders and artistic greats, from Gandhi to the Beatles, Henry VIII (with all his wives), to Bishop Desmond Tutu and Van Gogh. Have a portrait taken of yourself with the Queen.

There's an interactive celebrity attraction called **Blush**, where you can squeeze up to Britney Spears in a pole-dancing routine, try your hand at being a showbiz reporter, or have a celebrity make-over. If you fancy your chances as a chanteur, have a go at **Pop Idol**, with a 'fully interactive' Simon Cowell to tell you whether you're singing in tune or not. **Premiere Night** covers past and present stars: Chaplin, Tom Cruise, Bogart, Elvis, Marilyn and the gang are all there.

Most popular is the **Chamber of Horrors** (which you can bypass). Torture, dismemberment, and mass murderers such as Jack the Ripper are all here. Finally, there is the **Spirit of London**, a journey through history in miniaturized black cabs. The tour starts in the 16th century, then proceeds through the Plague, the Great Fire, the Victorian era, the Blitz and the Swinging Sixties.

Above: *Queen Elizabeth I, one of hundreds of wax dummies on display at the renowned Madame Tussaud's.*

Madame Tussaud's
✉ Marylebone Road, London NW1 5LR
☎ 0870 400 3000
📠 (020) 7465 0862
🖥 www. madame-tussauds.com (international)
🖥 www. madame-tussauds. co.uk (London)
⊖ Baker Street.
🕐 Mon–Fri 09:30–17:30, Sat–Sun 09:00–18:00
🔋 Visitors can buy joint tickets to Madame Tussauds and adjacent London Planetarium.
🍽 Coffee shop on site, wide range of facilities in Marylebone Road.

Right: *Cumberland Terrace, in Regent's Park, is an elegant example of Nash architecture.*

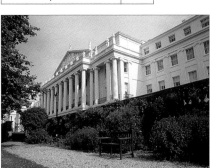

☉ *See* Map C–C1 | ★

REGENT'S PARK

Extending north from Marylebone Road up towards Hampstead and Camden, Regent's Park is best known as the home of **London Zoo** (*see* page 43), and for the elegant **Regency terraces** (designed by John Nash) surrounding it. It was a thickly wooded area (and the private hunting grounds of Henry VIII) until Cromwell felled most of its 1600 trees to help build ships for the Navy.

John Nash and the Prince Regent (later George IV) envisaged a belt of grand terraced houses around the outside of the park, and though never completed, Nash's legacy is still visible in the cream-coloured stucco of **Chester Terrace** and **Cumberland Terrace**, and the architecturally diverse houses of **Park Village West**. The **Open-Air Theatre** in the Inner Circle was popular in the 1930s for its productions of *A Midsummer Night's Dream*, and the summer repertoire still includes Shakespeare. Nearby **Queen Mary's Gardens** have one of the country's best rose displays. Beyond Prince Albert Row is **Primrose Hill**, well worth the climb to enjoy sweeping panoramas of the city.

Regent's Canal

Running in a meandering path through north and east London down to the Thames at Limehouse, **Regent's Canal** was completed in 1820 and is still in use by narrowboats today. One of the most attractive sections is the small basin known as **Little Venice**, in Maida Vale (⊖ Warwick Avenue) from where you can catch a **waterbus** down to **London Zoo** (which has its own jetty) and then down to **Camden Lock**. The service runs hourly on the hour ☉ Apr– Oct daily 10:00–17:00; Nov–Mar Sat–Sun 10:00–15:00. Details from the **London Waterbus Company**, ☎ (020) 7482 2550. **Jason's Canal Boats** do the same journey, with a commentary but without a zoo stop; ☎ (020) 7286 3428.

REGENT'S PARK & WINDSOR CASTLE

See Map A–C4 ★

WINDSOR CASTLE

This is the oldest and largest inhabited castle in England and official weekend residence of the Queen. Originally a timber and earth stronghold built by William the Conqueror, the castle grew in importance during Norman and Plantagenet times and was rebuilt in stone by Henry II. George IV added the **Round Tower** – a distinguishing feature – and many of the state apartments.

The **State Apartments** were badly damaged in a fire in 1992 but are fully restored to their former splendour. Amid the gilded ceilings and ornate furnishings are several important works by Rubens, Rembrandt and Van Dyck as well as superb Gobelin tapestries. Don't miss the exquisite **Queen Mary's Dolls House**, an amazing creation which took three years to complete. Designed by Edwin Lutyens in 1920, the house has working plumbing, lifts, and electricity. Nearby is the **Gallery**, which features themed exhibitions from the extensive Royal Collection of paintings, sculpture and objets d'art.

Passing through the Lower Ward you reach **St George's Chapel**, one of the finest ecclesiastical buildings in England, begun in 1475 by Edward IV. Ten British monarchs (including Henry VIII and his favourite wife, Jane Seymour) are buried here; one of the best times to visit the chapel is when the choir is singing evensong (at 17:15 daily).

Windsor Castle
✉ Windsor, Berkshire SL4 1NJ
☎ (020) 7766 7304
📠 (020) 7930 9625
📧 information@ royalcollection.org.uk
🖥 www.royal.gov.uk
🕐 Mar–Oct 09:45–17:15 (last entry 16:00); Nov–Feb 09:45–16:15 (last entry 15:00); closed 19 Jun, 7 Nov and 25–26 Dec. State Apartments closed 12–23 Jun and 30 Oct to 10 Nov. St. George's Chapel closed 16–19 Jun, 14 Oct from 13:00, 23 Dec from 13:00 and 24 Dec. St. George's Chapel also closed Sun except for worshippers.
💰 Admission is usually reduced when parts of the castle are closed.
🍴 Pubs and cafés in Windsor town centre.

Below: *Windsor Castle, viewed from the Long Walk.*

Above: *The ornately decorated ceiling of St Paul's Cathedral.*

London Central Mosque

Situated on the western edge of Regent's Park, the London Central Mosque attests to the continuing religious and architectural diversity of the capital. Completed in 1978, it has a shining copper dome, a minaret and traditional Islamic interior décor. It can accommodate up to 1800 worshippers. Non-Muslim visitors should start at the information centre.

Places of Worship
St Martin-in-the-Fields

Built in 1726, it has a fine Corinthian portico, topped by an unusual tower and steeple. The interior boasts an Italian plasterwork ceiling. The crypt has a brass-rubbing centre and a café. Evening concerts Thu–Sat, free lunch-hour concerts on Mon, Tue and Fri.

⊠ Trafalgar Square, London WC2
☎ (020) 7839 8362 (concerts), 7930 9306 (brass rubbing centre)
🖳 stmartin-in-the-fields.org
🕓 08:00–18:00 daily; brass rubbing centre 10:00–18:00 Mon–Sat, 12:00–18:00 Sun.
⊖ Charing Cross, Leicester Square

St James's Church

Built by Wren in 1684, it has a graceful interior and an ornate altar screen carved by the 17th-century master Grinling Gibbons. Pitt the Elder and William Blake were baptised in this church, which today hosts society weddings, lectures, and concerts, as well as ministering to the homeless and hosting markets.

⊠ 197 Piccadilly, London W1
☎ (020) 7734 4511
🖳 www.st-james-piccadilly.org
🕓 08:00–19:00 daily
⊖ Piccadilly Circus

St Bride's

Behind Reuters is St Bride's, designed by Wren and known as the 'journalists' church'. The crypt contains a small museum of Fleet Street history.

✉ Fleet Street, London EC4
☎ (020) 7427 0133
🕐 08:00–19:00, Sat 10:30–variable
⊖ St Paul's

St Anne's Church

Limehouse, where the city's first Chinese community settled, is home to this church, distinguished by its church clock: the highest in the City.

✉ Commercial Road, London E14 7HP
☎ (020) 7515 0977
🕐 by appointment
⊖ Canary Wharf

Southwark Cathedral

A cathedral only since 1905, the building is rich in history. It grew from a 13th-century church incorporating part of a Roman villa: an audio tour is available. Parts of a genuine archaeological dig can be seen in the passage between the cathedral and the *Long View of London* exhibition, which uses 21st-century technology to explore the past.

✉ Montagu Close, London SE1
☎ (020) 7367 6700
🕐 08:00–18:00 daily (closing times vary on religious holidays)
⊖ London Bridge

Other places of worship on pages 15, 17 and 33.

Museums & Galleries
Tate Britain

What was once the Tate Gallery is now Tate Britain, the non-British works having been transferred to Tate Modern (*see page 18*). Tate Britain houses the renowned Turner collection (some 282 paintings and 20,000 drawings, not all on display simultaneously), and is where works competing for the Turner prize are displayed.

✉ Millbank, SW1P 4RG
☎ (020) 7887 8000
🖥 www.tate.org.uk
🕐 10:00–17:50 daily
💲 free; charges for special exhibitions vary.
⊖ Pimlico, Vauxhall

London Transport Museum

This museum traces the history of transport in the city: old horse-drawn buses, trams, the underground (the world's oldest, begun in 1863), buses and much more. There are interactive exhibits (including a computer-simulated tube-train drive) and such things as old news items and posters can be viewed on computer screens.

✉ Covent Garden Piazza, WC2E 7BB
☎ (020) 7379 6344
🖥 www.ltmuseum.co.uk
🕐 10:00–17:15 Sat–Thu, 11:00–17:15 Fri
💲 Entrance charge
⊖ Covent Garden, Holborn, Leicester Square

Theatre Museum

This museum contains props, programmes and costumes from the world of ballet, theatre, circus and opera. There's also a display ('Slap') of the history of stage make-up. Demonstrations are given (between 11:30

The Geffrye Museum

Housed in early Georgian almshouses, this unusual museum offers a series of rooms and garden rooms depicting domestic styles of the urban middle classes from around 1600 to the present day.
🕐 Open 10:00–17:00 Tue–Sat, 12:00–17:00 Sun and holidays.
🔔 Admission is free. The museum is located in the northeast of London, at Kingsland Road, E2 (about 15 minutes' walk north of ⊖ Liverpool Street Station – there are also buses). For more information about exhibitions, workshops, performances, lectures and special events, visit the website: 🖥 www. geffrye-museum.org.uk

Bethnal Green Museum of Childhood

This museum, in Cambridge Heath Road, houses a superb collection of toys and games past and present, including teddy bears, doll's houses and puppets.
🕐 Open 10:00–17:50 Sat–Thu; 🖥 www. museumofchildhood. org.uk

and 16:30), and you may be picked for a theatrical face make-up. There are also daily costume workshops at 12:30 and 15:00.
✉ 1 Tavistock Street, WC2E 7PR
☎ (020) 7943 4700
🖥 www. theatremuseum.org
🕐 10:00–18:00 Tue–Sun, last entry 17:30 (closed bank holidays)
⊖ Covent Garden

Sir John Soane's Museum

This is one of London's best-kept secrets. Based on personal artworks and antiques of architect Sir John Soane, it has works by Turner, Hogarth, Reynolds and Canaletto, and many of his architectural drawings. In the basement of this intriguing house is the Egyptian sarcophagus of Seti I.
✉ 13 Lincoln's Inn Fields, WC2A 3BP
☎ (020) 7405 2107
🖥 www.soane.org
🕐 10:00–17:00 Tue–Sat, 18:00–21:00 (candle-lit) 1st Tue of month; tours 14:30 Sat

🔔 free, but donations welcome; there's a fee for Sat tours, free concessions.
⊖ Holborn

Museum of London

There are 14 galleries charting the history of London, starting with the new Prehistoric Gallery. The Roman Gallery showcases the Roman era, with archaeological finds from around the City, mosaics, sculptures, re-creations of a Roman street and the interior of ordinary houses, plus models of public baths, a forum and the old fort. On the same floor the tale continues through medieval times to the Great Fire of London in 1666. Highlights are the Cheapside Hoard (spectacular jewellery spanning centuries), a model of the Globe Theatre and the Great Fire Experience (small diorama with a tape of diarist Samuel Pepys's first-hand account). Downstairs (past the entrance to a lovely little Nursery Garden) the display begins with the Stuart period and continues to the 20th century. Exhibits here include costumes and music, recreated shops and offices, a pub, posters, paintings, an Art Deco lift from Selfridges and various carriages, including the gilded Lord Mayor's Coach. The museum presents lectures, films and special events.

✉ 150 London Wall, EC2Y 5HN
☎ (020) 7600 3699
💻 www.museumof london.org.uk
🕐 10:00–17:50 Mon–Sat, 12:00–17:50 Sun
💰 free, except for special exhibitions
⊖ Barbican, St Paul's

Whitechapel Art Gallery

This top contemporary art gallery in the heart of the East End was founded by a Victorian philanthropist and today often stages unusual exhibitions of avant-garde art from around the world.

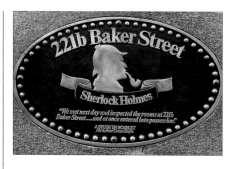

✉ 80–82 Whitechapel High Steet, E1 7QX
☎ (020) 7522 7878
💻 www. whitechapel.org
🕐 Tue–Sun 11:00–18:00, Thu 11:00–21:00, closed Mon.
💰 Admission free
⊖ Aldgate East

Sherlock Holmes Museum

The fictional Victorian detective, Sherlock Holmes, had his home at 221b Baker Street. This is a faithful reconstruction of his house as it might have been. It is, in fact, located at 239 Baker Street, though the sign on the door says otherwise.

✉ 221B Baker Street, London NW1
☎ (020) 7935 8866
💻 www.sherlock-holmes.co.uk

Above: *A plaque on the wall of 221b Baker Street marks the site of Sherlock Holmes's supposed address.*

Jewish Museum

Within a few minutes' walk of ⊖ Camden Town tube is the Jewish Museum, which has a series of stylish galleries on Jewish religious life and history in Britain, and a renowned ceremonial art collection; there are also interesting audiovisual displays explaining the Jewish faith and customs. It also contains treasures from London's **Great Synagogue** which was burnt down during World War II.

✉ 129 Albert Street
🕐 Open 10:00–15:30 Mon–Thu, 10:00–16:30 Sun; closed on bank and Jewish holidays.
💻 www. jewishmuseum.org.uk

Above: *St John's Gate is one of the three medieval establishments that survive today.*

Museum of Garden History

Next door to Lambeth Palace, inside a de-consecrated church are displays on the development of garden design and early plant hunters (such as 17th-century Royal Gardener, John Tradescant, who travelled widely to bring new species back to Britain). Outside, there is a period garden with, unexpectedly, the sarcophagus of Captain Bligh of *Mutiny on the Bounty* fame. ☺ Open 10:30–17:00 daily, Feb to mid-Dec.

☼ 09:30–18:00 (last admissions 17:30)
🛢 Entrance charge
⊖ Baker Street

Museum of the Order of St John

The remains of the 13th-century priory of the crusading Knights Hospitallers are south-east of Clerkenwell Green. The most con-spicuous remnant is St John's Gate. To see the Grand Priory crypt, the Gatehouse and Chapter Hall, you must join a tour.

✉ St John's Gate, St John's Lane, EC1
☎ (020) 7324 4000
🖳 www.sja.org.uk/history
☼ 09:00–17:00 Mon–Fri, 10:00–16:00 Sat; tours 11:00, 14:30 Tue, Fri, Sat.
🛢 Admission free
⊖ Farringdon

Imperial War Museum

From the trenches of Flanders to the hi-tech Gulf War, modern war-fare is presented. The main gallery features tanks, V2 rockets, a Spitfire and a Polaris missile. Interactive exhibits include walk-through World War I trenches (with mud, rats and simulated shellfire), a recreated Blitz scenario in the bomb-ravaged streets of wartime London, and the Secret War (about spies). The Holocaust Exhibition is a harrowing audio-visual depiction of the Nazi campaign against all undesirables, with inevitable concentra-tion on the Jews, and includes a scale model of Auschwitz. The latest addition covers the charismatic war-time leader 'Monty'.

✉ Lambeth Road, SE1 6HZ
☎ (020) 7416 5320
🖳 www.iwm.org.uk
☼ 10:00–18:00 daily
🛢 Admission free
⊖ Elephant & Castle

Florence Nightingale Museum

On a corner of St Thomas's Hospital is a small museum devoted to the indefatigable 'Lady with the Lamp', with audiovisual presentations and recreations of the Crimean military hospitals where she earned her reputation as heroine.

✉ *2 Lambeth Palace Road, SE1 7EN*
☎ *(020) 7620 0374*
🖳 *www.florence-nightingale.co.uk*
🕐 *10:00–17:00 Mon–Fri (last entry 16:00); 11:30–16:30 Sat–Sun (last entry 15:30).*
🎒 *Under 5s free*
⊖ *Westminster, Waterloo*

Dalí Universe

This intriguing museum (entrance on the river side of County Hall) has a collection of bizarre paintings, sculptures, graphics, jewellery and furniture created by eccentric Spanish Surrealist Salvador Dalí: a must for aficionados and also fascinating for non-fans.

✉ *County Hall, Queen's Walk, SE1 7PB*
☎ *(020) 7620 2720*
🖳 *www.daliuniverse.com*
🕐 *10:00–17:30 daily*
🎒 *Under 4s free*
⊖ *Waterloo*

National Maritime Museum

The Nelson Gallery has the coat Nelson was wearing at the Battle of Trafalgar (with the hole made by the musket ball that killed him, and also the ball itself). Turner's *Victory of the Battle of Trafalgar* features commentary and simulation of the battle. In the interactive All Hands gallery you can try out your seafaring skills.

✉ *Romney Road, SE10*
☎ *(020) 8858 4422*
🖳 *www.nmm.ac.uk*
🕐 *10:00–17:00 daily (last admission 16:30)*
🎒 *Admission free*
⊖ *DLR Greenwich or Cutty Sark*

Other museums and galleries on pages 16, 18, 20 and 23.

Bramah Museum of Tea and Coffee

Situated in Southwark Street is an interesting little museum covering three centuries of the social and commercial history of the world's two favourite hot beverages. After admiring the exhibits, including several teapots in a variety of amusing designs, you can sample the brew of your choice in the small café on the premises, where traditional English afternoon tea is served 14:00–16:00. 🕐 Open daily 10:00–18:00; 🖳 www.bramahmuseum.co.uk

Clink Prison Museum

Clink Prison is a small but atmospheric recreation in what remains of a real 12th-century prison, which has given its name as a slang term for all prisons. The guided tour is recommended. 🕐 Mon–Fri 10:00–18:00, Sat–Sun 10:00–20:00; 🖳 www.clink.co.uk

Chelsea Physic Garden
One of the great delights of Chelsea is this little-known garden in Royal Hospital Road. It marks the beginning of Cheyne Walk and is the second oldest botanical garden in England after Oxford's. It was founded by the Society of Apothecaries in 1673 and used to teach physicians the medicinal uses of plants and herbs from all over the world. The Chelsea Physic Garden contains over 5000 plants. At the entrance, maps are available with a list of the most interesting flowers and shrubs.
🕘 12:00–17:00 Wed, 14:00–18:00 Sun Apr–Oct. 🖳 www.chelsea physicgarden.co.uk

Below: *A view of the Thames from Richmond. Easily accessible from the city centre, Richmond, with its famous park, has a lot to offer visitors.*

Parks and Gardens

Richmond Park

Charles I hunted here and enclosed the park within a wall (still there) in the 17th century. At 1000ha (2471 acres) it is easily the largest city park in Europe. Much of it is natural wilderness, except the landscaped plantations of rhododendron and azaleas, which give gorgeous displays in spring. Red and fallow deer roam the park, and there is plenty of bird life (particularly in Sidmouth Wood, which is a bird sanctuary).
✉ Richmond, Surrey
☎ (020) 8948 3209
🕘 07:30–dusk Aug–Apr, 07:30–21:00 May–Jul
🔓 Admission free
⊖ Richmond

Holland Park

This charming park covers just 22ha (54 acres) but has woodland areas (best in May, when azaleas and rhododendrons are in bloom), rose gardens, formal flower gardens, an iris garden and a Japanese garden (created for the 1991 London Festival of Japan). It was once the garden of 17th-century Holland House, largely destroyed in World War II. The remains of the house now contain a youth hostel and restaurant; the terrace is used as an open-air theatre in summer. In Holland Park Road is Leighton House, crammed with art treasures.
✉ Leighton House, 12 Holland Park Road, W18 8LZ
☎ (020) 7602 3316
🖳 www.rbkc.gov.uk/ leigthonhousemuseum
🕘 07:30–dusk (park), 11:00–17:15 Wed–Sun (Leighton House)
🔓 Admission free
⊖ High Street Kensington

Left: *Wimbledon is the setting for the prestigious lawn tennis championship: one of the sport's four Grand Slam events.*

ACTIVITIES
Sport and Recreation

London offers opportunities for the sporty to take part in all sorts of activities, ranging from aerobics to windsurfing. Council-run facilities provide inexpensive access to sports such as tennis, swimming, weight-training, aerobics and so on. There are also numerous private gymnasiums and health clubs, including some in major hotels. The parks, of course, offer opportunities for jogging, walking, tennis or boating.

Football (soccer) probably arouses more passion in the English than any other game, and although it is usually the big northern clubs which dominate the league tables, London prides itself on the strength of its teams such as Arsenal (the Gunners), Tottenham Hotspur (Spurs) and Chelsea. The season is from mid-August to early May, culminating in the FA Cup Final at Wembley Stadium.

Climax of the international **tennis** season is the Grand Slam tournament, played on the famous grass courts at Wimbledon in the last week of June and the first week of July. Almost as famous for the cost of off-court strawberries as for the on-court antics

---

Sporting Venues

Tickets for major international sporting events can be extremely hard to come by, and you need to book well in advance (sometimes several months). Here are some useful telephone numbers:
Crystal Palace National Sports Centre,
☎ (020) 8778 0131;
Lord's Cricket Ground,
☎ (020) 7289 1611;
The Oval,
☎ (020) 7582 6660;
Ascot Racecourse,
☎ (01344) 622 211;
Epsom Downs,
☎ (01372) 726 311;
Kempton Park,
☎ (01932) 782 292;
Sandown Park,
☎ (01372) 464 348;
Windsor,
☎ (01753) 498 400;
Twickenham Stadium,
☎ (020) 8831 6666;
Wimbledon All England Lawn Tennis Club,
☎ (020) 8946 2244.

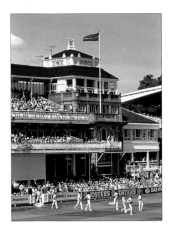

Above: *Lord's Cricket Ground, in St John's Wood, is one of London's most famous sporting venues.* **Opposite:** *Snowdon Aviary, alongside Regent's Canal at London Zoo.*

London Marathon
Held in March/April, the **Flora London Marathon** follows a 40km (25-mile) course from Greenwich to Westminster and attracts around 30,000 participants annually. To participate, you must book before the end of September in the previous year. Details from the marathon hotline, ☎ (020) 7902 0189; 🖳 www. london-marathon.co.uk

of the international stars, tickets for the 'Wimbledon fortnight' are notoriously hard to obtain.

The **cricket** season runs from Apr–Sep. England's love of cricket is best appreciated on a sunny weekend afternoon, from a traditional pub overlooking the village green. Although dominated by arcane rules and peculiar terminology ('yorkers', 'googlies', 'silly mid-offs' and so on), cricket can arouse fierce rivalry. The biggest drawcards of the season are the international test matches between England and touring teams, one of which is always played at Lord's Cricket Ground (the home of the Middlesex County Cricket Club), and another at The Oval.

Major international **athletics** events, as well as local contests, take place at the Crystal Palace National Sports Centre, with the two biggest competitions in early summer (Jun–Jul) and late summer (Aug).

Horse racing provides an insight into the personalities of the British people. Major race courses within easy reach of London include Ascot (the Royal Ascot meeting in June), Epsom (Derby Day in June), Kempton Park, Sandown Park, and Windsor.

Two kinds of **rugby** are played in Britain: Rugby Union (15-a-side) and Rugby League (13-a-side). London has one Rugby League team (the London Broncos), with other major teams (such as the Wasps, Harlequins and London Irish) playing Rugby Union. The season (Sep–Apr/May) culminates in the Pilkington Cup, held at the end of April at Twickenham Stadium in West London.

Fun for Children
London Zoo

London Zoo has long been at the forefront of zoological studies and scientific research into animal genetics, ecology, behaviour, and reproduction, and can claim many firsts, including the public **aquarium** (1849), the **reptile house** (1853), the **insect house** (1881), and a **children's zoo** (1938).

The complex contains twelve structures, including **Mappin Terraces** (resembles a mountain landscape for sloth bears and other animals), the much-loved **penguin pool**, **giraffe house** and **Snowdon Aviary**.

The zoo has over 600 species, from the tiniest (and endangered) tree snails in the invertebrate house to the elegant giraffes. Kids can feed and handle animals in the **Ambika Paul Children's Zoo**, see pelicans and penguins being fed, peer at possums and other creatures of the night in **Moonlight World** and watch a variety of birds and animals show off their special skills in the **Animals in Action** presentation.

Planetarium

The Planetarium, next door to **Madame Tussaud's** (*see* page 31), is equally popular and covered by the same ticket. As well as the main show, the **Planetarium** has exhibitions with models of planets, satellites and spacecraft (many of them interactive). The main 10-minute space show uses images from spacecraft and satellites woven together with a narrative on space travel, planets and the stars. It begins every 20–30 minutes.

London Zoo
✉ Regents Park, NW1 4RY
☎ (020) 7722 3333
🖥 www.londonzoo.co.uk
🕐 10:00–17:30 Mar–Oct, 10:00–16:00 Nov–Feb (last entry 1 hour before closing).
🎫 Under 3s free
⊖ Camden Town, or Baker Street then 274 or C2 bus

Planetarium
✉ Marleybone Road, NW1
☎ 0870 400 3000
🖥 www.madame-tussauds.com
🕐 10:00–17:00 daily Jun–Aug, 12:30–17:00 Mon–Fri, 10:00–17:00 Sat–Sun, Sep–May.
🎫 combined ticket with Madame Tussaud's
⊖ Baker Street

HMS Belfast
✉ Morgan's Lane, Tooley Street, SE1 2JH
☎ (020) 7940 6300
🖥 www.iwm.org.uk/belfast
🕐 daily 10:00–18:00 Mar–Oct, 10:00–17:00 Nov–Feb (last admission 45 mins before closing).
⊖ London Bridge, Tower Bridge

The London Dungeon
✉ 28–34 Tooley
Street, London SE1 2SZ
☎ (020) 7403 7221
🖵 www.
thedungeons.com
🕐 10:00–17:30
Apr–Sep, 10:30–17:30
Oct–Mar
⊖ London Bridge

The Changing of the Guard
This free spectacle on the forecourt of Buckingham Palace still draws in the crowds. The New Guard marches from Wellington Barracks to arrive at the Palace just after 11:30, and the band plays while the keys are ceremonially handed over. The Old Guard then returns to the barracks, leaving the Palace in the hands of the New Guard till the following morning. The ceremony takes place 🕐 daily May–Aug, on alternate days Sep–Apr; it may be cancelled in wet weather.

Below: *The grisly London Dungeon attracts vast crowds.*

HMS Belfast

The largest surviving battle cruiser from World War II, *HMS Belfast* remained in service until 1965 and is now a floating museum, moored just upstream from Tower Bridge. This complex warship (which carried 800 crew) has nine decks and you can explore all of it, from the bridge down to the engine and boiler rooms. (For contact details, *see* panel, page 43.)

The London Dungeon

Not for the faint-hearted or very young, older children will certainly enjoy the London Dungeon. Housed in vaults on Tooley Street, the dungeon is a macabre look at the gruesome aspects of history, with life-size tableaux (some animatronic) of people being beheaded, drawn and quartered, hanged, etc. It ends with a boat ride through Traitor's Gate, leading to a tour of Jack the Ripper's London and a recreation of the Great Fire of London. The dungeon is immensely popular, so be prepared to queue for some time.

Other Attractions for Children

Children enjoy the **London Eye** (*see* page 22), the **Changing of the Guard** at Buckingham Palace (*see* page 24 and also panel, this page), the **Tower of London** (*see* page 19), **Greenwich** (*see* page 28), the **London Transport Museum** (*see* page 35), the **Sherlock Holmes Museum** (*see* page 37) and the **South Kensington museums** (*see* page 23).

Alternative London

Greyhound Racing

For a night out with a difference, you could attend a greyhound racing meeting – it doesn't cost an arm and a leg and is very entertaining. The stadiums around London all have restaurants, some of which are very good. Greyhound racing has become such a popular pursuit that it is advisable to book ahead if you want to watch the races from a restaurant table.

Meetings usually consist of about a dozen races, and the excitement runs high. There are six dogs in each race, whizzing down the track at amazing speeds. To add to the rush, you could place a bet on your favourite dog – but don't wager more than you can afford!

For more details, including information about the specific race tracks, the history of greyhound racing and also some interesting information about the breed itself, visit the excellent website of the **British Greyhound Racing Board** (*see* panel, this page).

The Freud Museum

If you're interested in something a little out of the ordinary, you can pay a visit to the Freud Museum. Housed in what was once the home of Sigmund Freud, and after his death the home of his daughter Anna, it contains Freud's extensive reference library and a wonderful collection of antiquities from Egypt, Greece, the Roman Empire and the East. There is a fascinating collection of fine furniture, including the most famous piece – the couch on which Freud's patients reclined. The museum also has research and educational programmes.

**The British Grey-
hound Racing Board**
💻 www.thedogs.co.uk

**Walthamstow
Stadium**
✉ Chingford Road,
London E4 8SJ
☎ (020) 8498 3300
(enquiries)
☎ (020) 8498 3333
(restaurant bookings)
✆ mail@
wsgreyhound.co.uk
💻 www.
wsgreyhound.co.uk
🕓 Tue, Thu and Sat
18:30 (evening race
meetings), Mon 12:30
and Fri 10:30 (lunch-
time meetings), closed
Good Friday and
Christmas Day.
👶 under 15s free.

**Wimbledon Stadium
(reservations)**
✉ c/o Belle Vue
Greyhound Stadium,
Kirkmanshulme Lane,
Gorton, Manchester
M18 7BA
☎ (020) 8946 8000
📞 0870 880 0123
✆ wmreserve@
gralimited.co.uk
💻 www.wimbledon
stadium.co.uk
🕓 08:30–18:00
Mon–Fri, 09:00–17:00
Sat, closed Sun.

Freud Museum
✉ 20 Maresfield Gar-
dens, London NW3 5SX
☎ (020) 7435 2002 or
(020) 7435 5267
📞 (020) 7431 5452
✆ freud@ gn.apc.org
💻 www.freud.org.uk
🚇 Finchley Road
🕓 12:00–17:00 Wed–
Sat, closed Mon–Tue.

Above: *Downing Street has been the residence of prime ministers since the mid-18th century.*

More Walking Tours
Tailor-made themed tours are available. For instance, you can take a 'Jack the Ripper' tour which focuses on the East End, an 'off-beat Soho' tour, an 'actor and authors' tour of Covent Garden, or a pub walk around Shakespeare and Dickens' London. Contact Tour Guides, ☎ 079 5738 8280; 🖳 www.tourguides.org.uk

Original London Walks is London's oldest established walking tour company, which features a varied programme of over 40 walks on different themes, ☎ (020) 7624 3978.

Walking Tours
Whitehall and Westminster

Starting off at **Trafalgar Square** (*see* page 16), which is reached via the Charing Cross tube station, proceed south along Whitehall. Lined with buildings housing key government offices and ministries, this avenue was named after the former Whitehall Palace, where Henry VIII lived for his last years. The palace was destroyed by fire in 1698, and only the **Banqueting House** (🕘 10:00–16:30, Mon–Sat), which was built by Inigo Jones for James I, remains. The wonderful ceiling in the main dining hall was painted by Rubens.

Opposite the Banqueting House is the **Horse Guards**, once the old palace guard house, where the troopers of the Queen's Household Cavalry stand outside their sentry boxes or on horseback. This is where the celebrated **Changing of the Guard** (see page 44) takes place.

Past the **Old Treasury** (on the same side of Whitehall as the Horse Guards) is the home of the British Prime Minister. **No. 10 Downing Street** was presented to Britain's first Prime Minister, Sir Robert Walpole, in 1732, and remained the PM's residence until Tony Blair took over No. 11, traditionally home of the Chancellor of the Exchequer.

Just south of Downing Street you will see the **Cenotaph**. Erected in 1919 to commemorate those who lost their lives during World War I, it is the focus of the Remembrance Sunday ceremony in November.

Just down King Charles Street off Whitehall's west side are the **Cabinet War Rooms** (🕘 daily 09:30–17:15 May–Sep, 10:00–17:15

Oct–Apr), underground headquarters of Churchill, the War Cabinet and Chiefs of Staff during World War II bombing raids. They include Churchill's bedroom, study and the Map Room (*see* picture, page 9).

Further south, at the end of Whitehall, is **Parliament Square**, where you will find **Westminster Abbey** (*see* page 15), **Big Ben** and the **Houses of Parliament** (*see* page 14).

If you are feeling particularly energetic, continue going south along Milbank until you reach **Tate Britain** (*see* page 35), after which you could go via **Buckingham Palace** (*see* page 24) and **St James's Park** (*see* Map D–B4/C4) back to Trafalgar Square.

> **Whitehall and Westminster**
> **Location:** Map D–C3
> **Distance:** about 1km (.62 mile)
> **Duration:** 40 minutes (not counting visits)
> **Start:** Trafalgar Square
> **Finish:** Houses of Parliament
>
> **South Bank**
> **Location:** Map D–E4
> **Distance:** about 3.5km (2 miles)
> **Duration:** 2–3 hours
> **Start:** Waterloo
> **Finish:** St Paul's Cathedral

South Bank

Starting from **Waterloo Station** (*see* Map D–E4), make your way south on York Road until you reach Westminster Bridge and Old County Hall, which is home to the **London Aquarium** (*see* page 22) and the amazing **Dalí Universe** (*see* page 39). Walk in a northerly direction along the promenade until you reach the **London Eye** (*see* page 22), from which you can see a magnificent panorama of the city.

Continuing along the promenade, with its wonderful river views, you will reach the **South Bank Centre** (*see* page 71), one of the main cultural hubs of the city. It is home to the Royal Festival Hall, Queen Elizabeth Hall and the Purcell Room. A little further along are the National Film

Below: *Salvador Dalí's surreal version of a love seat: the marvellous* Mae West Lips Sofa, *which can be seen at Dalí Universe.*

River Boat Operators
Westminster Passenger Services (cruises upriver from Westminster to Hampton Court, via Kew and Richmond), ☎ (020) 7930 2062
Catamaran Cruisers (cruises from Embankment, Waterloo and Westminster to Greenwich or the Tower), ☎ (020) 7987 1185
Thames River Services (from Westminster to the Tower or Greenwich – some boats continuing to the Thames Barrier), ☎ (020) 7930 4097
City Cruises (hop-on hop-off between Waterloo and Greenwich, including stop at the Tower, with Red Rover day ticket), ☎ (020) 7740 0400
London Showboat (cabaret and dinner cruise to Thames Barrier from Westminster), ☎ (020) 7740 0400
Bateaux London (lunch and dinner cruises from Embankment), ☎ (020) 7925 2215

Theatre, the Royal National Theatre, BFI Film Centre and the London Television Centre.

Past Gabriel's Wharf is the **Oxo Tower Wharf**, which offers a rooftop restaurant – ☎ (020) 7803 3888 – as well as a bar and brasserie noted for fabulous views. It also contains unusual design stores (⏱ 11:00–18:00 Tue–Sun) selling unique products, and a gallery with a changing programme of design-based exhibitions (⏱ 11:00–18:00 daily). For a free directory of events in and around Oxo Tower, ☎ (020) 7410 3610.

Continue walking along the promenade, which now goes in an easterly direction, until you reach **Tate Modern** (*see* page 18) and **Shakespeare's Globe** (*see* page 26). Once you have spent a while at these attractions and caught your breath, you can cross to the north bank of the Thames via the **Millennium Bridge** (*see* page 18) and keep going north until you end up at **St Paul's Cathedral** (*see* page 17).

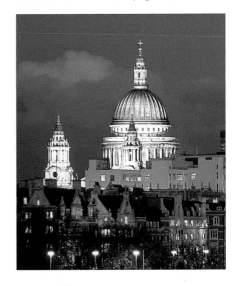

Right: *The dome of St Paul's Cathedral dominates the city skyline by night.*

Organized Tours

The **London Tourist Board** (LTB) does not run a telephone enquiry service, but there is an automated 24-hour London Line. Calls cost 60p per minute and you should have pen and paper handy. This service provides information on museums,

Above: *The Official London Sightseeing Boat is a good way to see the sights along the Thames.*

galleries, attractions, river boats, tours, accommodation, theatre, what's on, Changing of the Guard, children's London, shopping, eating out and gay/lesbian London.

Double-decker hop-on hop-off sightseeing tours are a good introduction to London, providing background information and various special offers, including tickets for attractions that enable you to queue-jump. Tickets are valid for 24 hours and you can get on and off at any stop. The two main companies (Big Bus and The Original Tour) have frequent services and stops that are convenient for the sights. Most vehicles have open top decks.

Itineraries tailored to your interests and personalized service are some advantages of a driver-guided tour. Try **Black Taxi Tours of London**, **British Tours** or **Take a Guide**.

The London **registered guides** have all undertaken rigorous training, after which they are issued with the coveted Blue Badge and photocard licence. **Professional Guide Services** and **Tours Guides International** are two companies that can book Blue Badge guides for anything from general sightseeing to special interest tours.

For a selection of **river boat operators**, *see* panel on page 48. For **canal boats**, try **Jason's Canal Boat** and **London Waterbus**.

Useful numbers
London Tourist Board
☎ (09068) 66 33 44
🖳 www.visitlondon.com
Big Bus
☎ (020) 7233 9533
The Original Tour
☎ (020) 8877 1722
Black Taxi Tours of London
☎ (020) 7935 9363
British Tours
☎ (020) 7734 8734
Take a Guide
☎ (020) 8960 0459
Professional Guide Services
☎ (020) 8874 2745
Tours Guides International
☎ (020) 7495 5504
Jason's Canal Boat
☎ (020) 7286 3428
London Waterbus
☎ (020) 7482 2550
or 24-hour recording
☎ (020) 7482 2660

Above: *The food hall at Harrods, where the emphasis is on quality.*
Opposite: *Floris in Jermyn Street, purveyors of fine fragrances since 1730.*

Shopping

Napoleon dubbed the English a 'nation of shopkeepers' and London has something for everyone, whatever your tastes or your budget.

Department Stores
Fortnum and Mason

An epicurean emporium which supplies delicacies to the Royal household, and magnificent picnic hampers for society events.
⊠ *181 Piccadilly, W1,*
☎ *(020) 7734 8040,* ⊕ *10:00–18:30, Mon–Sat.*

Harrods

With 300 departments spread over seven floors, this is a store which actually imposes a dress code: no shorts, ripped jeans or vest tops are allowed. Don't miss the Art Deco food halls on the ground floor.
⊠ *87 Brompton Road, SW1,* ☎ *(020) 7730 1234,* ⊕ *10:00–19:00, Mon–Sat.*

Harvey Nichols

Known as 'Harvey Nicks' to its regular customers, this is another one of London's top department stores.
⊠ *102–125 Knightsbridge, SW1,*
☎ *(020) 7235 5000,* ⊕ *10:00– 20:00 Mon–Fri, 10:00–19:00 Sat.*

John Lewis

'Never knowlingly undersold' is their famous motto.
⊠ *278–306 Oxford Street, W1,* ☎ *(020) 7629 7711,* ⊕ *09:30–19:00 Mon–Sat, 09:30–20:00 Thu, 12:00–18:00 Sun.*

Late-night Shopping
Late-night shopping varies from area to area (n Kensington High Street, Oxford Street and Covent Garden it is on Thursdays; in Knightsbridge and Chelsea it's Wednesdays) with shops open until 19:00 or 20:00. Many shops are also open longer hours during the month before Christmas.

Liberty

One of London's most exclusive department stores, Liberty is especially famous for its fabric designs.

✉ 212–299 Regent Street, W1, ☎ (020) 7734 1234, ⊕ 10:00–19:00 Mon–Wed and Fri, 10:00–20:00 Thu, 10:00–19:00 Sat, 12:00–18:00 Sun.

Marks & Spencer

This store offers consistent good quality, albeit sometimes a little dull.

✉ 458 Oxford Street, W1, ☎ (020) 7935 7954, ⊕ 09:00–21:00 Mon–Fri, 08:30–20:00 Sat, 12:00–18:00 Sun.

Selfridges

This department store is one of the great landmarks of Oxford Street, the elegant Edwardian building being noted especially for its imposing colonnaded façade.

✉ 400 Oxford Street, W1, ☎ 0870 837 7377, ⊕ 10:00–20:00 Mon–Fri, 09:30–20:00 Sat, 12:00–18:00 Sun.

Shops
Oxford Street and Surrounds

Almost a mile long, Oxford Street may be one of the best shopping streets in the capital but the stretch east of Oxford Circus is rather tawdry, filled with tacky souvenir shops and cut-price clothing. The stretch west of Oxford Circus contains most of the more upmarket establishments and is home to major chains and department stores such as Selfridges, Marks & Spencer, John Lewis, Debenhams Next, and Allders, as well as mega-media stores such as HMV and Virgin. North of Oxford Street, St Christopher's Place features numerous designer outlets, while on the opposite side, South Molton Street is another popular area for fashion boutiques. Off Oxford Street, Bond Street and New Bond Street have quality fashions, haute couture, art galleries, jewellery (including Asprey & Garrard) and antique shops. Leading down from Oxford Circus to Piccadilly, Regent Street is home to Liberty's department store, Laura Ashley, Hamleys toyshop, several crystal and china shops, a Disney store, Dickins & Jones, and also classic British clothing shops such as Aquascutum, Jaeger and Austin Reed. East of Regent Street, Carnaby Street was world famous in the 'Swinging Sixties' but is now full of tacky souvenir shops. Parallel to Regent Street on its west side, Savile Row is well known as the best place to go for bespoke tailoring.

Piccadilly and St James's

Piccadilly Circus features the indoor shopping complexes of the Trocadero and London Pavilion, as well as Lillywhites, the sports department store, and the vast Tower Records. Piccadilly is lined with car showrooms and airline offices but has some famous shops such as Fortnum and Mason, and Hatchards (books). South of Piccadilly in St James's is Jermyn Street, which has numerous small, old-fashioned shops offering exciting finds such as fine handmade shoes. On the north side of Piccadilly, the Burlington Arcade is another old-fashioned enclave with quality shops selling everything from porcelain to antique jewellery, Irish linen and cashmere jumpers.

Knightsbridge, Kensington and Chelsea

One of the most expensive shopping areas in the capital, Knightsbridge features classy boutiques and designer fashion shops, and world-famous Harrods. Sloane Street, with Harvey Nichols and yet more expensive clothing outlets, leads into Sloane Square and the beginning of King's Road. Once one of London's great fashion meccas, King's Road can still hold its own, with many trendy designer outlets. Kensington has antique shops along Kensington Church Street, department stores and clothes boutiques on Kensington High Street, and a cluster of British-based design outlets, with superb windows, in Beauchamp Place.

Covent Garden and Soho

Covent Garden has an eclectic mix of shops, selling virtually everything from designer clothes to arts, crafts, books, antiques and more. To the north of Covent Garden, Floral Street is hot on street fashions, while Neal's Yard tends to be the focus for 'alternative'

goods and whole-foods. Alongside the pornographic outlets in Soho there are unusual specialist shops, from Continental delicatessens to small record shops. Between Soho and Covent Garden, Charing Cross Road is synonymous with the book trade, with numerous specialized outlets (for both new and second-hand books), and major bookstores such as Foyle (No. 119) and Waterstones (No. 121).

Markets
Brick Lane Market
Bric-a-brac, fruit and veg, clothes and more.
⊠ *near Spitalfields E1,* ⊕ *Sun 08:00–13:00*

Camden Market
120 stalls, mostly fashion, jewellery, great second-hand clothing, music and food.
⊠ *Camden Town,* ⊕ *09:00–17:30 Thu–Sun.*

Camden Lock
Bric-a-brac, candles, prints, books, period clothing and more.

⊠ *Camden Town,* ⊕ *10:00–18:00 Sat, Sun; indoor stalls 10:00–18:00 daily.*

Portobello Road
From CDs to antiques, one of the city's best-loved markets.
⊠ *Portobello Rd, W10,* ⊕ *general 10:00–17:00 Mon–Fri;* ⊕ *antiques 06:00–17:00 Sat).*

Greenwich
This market sells mostly bric-a-brac, arts, crafts, clothes.
⊠ *College Approach, SE10,*
☎ *(020) 7515 7153,* ⊕ *09:30–17:00 Fri–Sun*

Petticoat Lane
Sells clothes, bric-a-brac, and more.
⊠ *Middlesex and Wentworth Streets, E1,* ⊕ *best between 09:00 and 14:00 Sun*

Above: *Portobello Road is one of London's biggest and busiest antique markets.*
Opposite: *Built in the 19th century, Burlington Arcade houses many small and exclusive shops.*

Camden Passage
Islington's main tourist attraction is the **antiques market**, which is located just a few minutes' walk from ⊖ Angel tube. It fills Camden Passage on Wednesday mornings and Saturdays, but the surrounding antique shops are open every day of the week.
Chapel Market, on the other side of Upper Street, is a traditional London flea market. It is open Tue–Sun.

Above: *The Dorchester Hotel, a London landmark.*

Hotel Chains
The big international hotel chains won't give you the same degree of individuality that characterizes the city's more famous hotels, but they offer the same consistent standards of service that they do elsewhere in the world. The luxurious **Four Seasons** chain (💻 www.fourseasons.com) has properties on Park Lane and at Canary Wharf (*see* page 58). **Sheraton** (💻 www.starwood.com/sheraton) has six properties, including two at Heathrow. **Hilton** (💻 www.hilton.com) has 13 properties in the centre, including Park Lane (*see* page 55). **Mariott** (💻 www.marriott.com) has about the same number. **Holiday Inn** (💻 www.holiday-inn.com) is also well represented at the budget end of the scale.

WHERE TO STAY

There's no getting around the fact that accommodation costs are going to make a large dent in your travel budget (now is the time to call in those favours from long-lost friends or distant relatives!). The problem is that London has a shortage of affordable, good quality accommodation, and even the renowned British **B&Bs** (bed & breakfast establishments) can seem eyewateringly expensive when they're near the centre of the city. Cheap options tend to be limited to backpackers' hostels or student residences – although the founder of **easyjet** has now promised that low-cost **easyhotels** are just around the corner.

What London does do well is to provide some really great **hotels**, and truly memorable experiences, if you're prepared to splash out. At the top end of the market there is a huge amount of choice, ranging from classy olde-worlde establishments to achingly hip boutique hotels.

Whatever your budget, plan as much in advance as you can. Don't even think of turning up in peak season (June–August) without a booking.

Most of the seriously classy hotels are concentrated around Mayfair and Knightsbridge; Covent Garden is a great area for boutique hotels close to the shopping and the theatre; Bloomsbury is also close to theatre land, and good for mid-priced hotels; Bayswater, Earl's Court and Victoria are the places to look for budget deals.

The West End

• *LUXURY*

Claridge's (Map D–A2)
A favourite with super-stars and royalty. Good service, but expensive.
✉ Brook Street, London W1, ☎ 020 7629 8860, 🖷 020 7499 2210, 🖰 info@claridges.co.uk 🖥 www.the-savoy-group.com

The Dorchester (Map C–D4)
A landmark, overlooking Hyde Park, popular with movie stars.
✉ 53 Park Lane, London W1, ☎ 020 7629 8888, 🖷 020 7409 0114, 🖰 info@dorchesterhotel.com 🖥 www.dorchesterhotel.com

London Hilton on Park Lane (Map D–A4)
Excellent views of Hyde Park; impeccable service, superb décor.
✉ 22 Park Lane, London W1, ☎ 020 7493 8000, 🖷 020 7208 4142, 🖰 reservations.parklane@hilton.com 🖥 www.hilton.com

The Ritz (Map D–B3)
Steeped in history, it has opulent Louis XVI décor with the west-facing rooms (facing Green Park) the best ones to book.
✉ 150 Piccadilly, London W1, ☎ 020 7493 8181, 🖷 020 7493 2687, 🖰 enquire@theritzlondon.com 🖥 www.theritzlondon.com

Metropolitan (Map D–A4)
Trendy Hyde Park hotel with spacious, well-equipped rooms and a great health club; its Met Bar is renowned as a busy hang-out for celebs and starlets.
✉ Old Park Lane, London W1, ☎ 020 7447 1000, 🖷 020 7447 1147, 🖰 res@metropolitan.co.uk 🖥 www.metropolitan.co.uk

No 5 Maddox Street (Map D–B2)
Luxurious, all-suites designer hotel with beautiful, serene Eastern-inspired rooms in the heart of Mayfair.
✉ 5 Maddox Street, London W1, ☎ 020 7647 0200, 🖷 020 7647 0300, 🖰 no5maddoxstreet@living-rooms.co.uk 🖥 www.living-rooms.co.uk

The Lanesborough (Map C–D5)
Housed in a former hospital, this is one of the city's best hotels with top-of-the-range rooms furnished in Regency style.
✉ Hyde Park Corner, SW1, ☎ 020 7259 5599, 🖷 020 7259 5606, 🖰 info@lanesborough.com 🖥 www.lanesborough.com

• *MID-RANGE*

The Goring (Map D–A5)
Well-located, family-run hotel with elegant public rooms and spacious en-suite bedrooms.
✉ 15 Beeston Place, London SW1, ☎ 020 7396 9000, 🖷 020 7834 4393, 🖰 reception@goringhotel.co.uk 🖥 www.goringhotel.co.uk

Hazlitt's (Map D–C2)

Period-style rooms in the 18th-century home of the essayist William Hazlitt.

✉ 6 Frith Street, London W1, ☎ 020 7434 1771, 📠 020 7439 1524, 🖰 reservations@hazlitts.co.uk 🖵 www.hazlittshotel.com

Bloomsbury and Covent Garden

• *LUXURY*

The Savoy (Map D–D3)

Top service and luxury; spacious rooms decorated in Art Deco style; good fitness centre.

✉ Strand, London WC2, ☎ 020 7950 5492, 📠 020 7950 5482, 🖰 reservations@the-savoy.co.uk 🖵 www.savoygroup.com

Charlotte Street Hotel (Map D–B1)

Well-situated hotel; beautifully styled bedrooms with full multi-media facilities.

✉ 15 Charlotte Street, W1, ☎ 020 7806 2000, 📠 020 7806 2002, 🖰 charlotte@firmdale.com 🖵 www.firmdale.com

• *MID-RANGE*

Radisson Edwardian Mountbatten (Map D–C2)

Country-house-style hotel in Covent Garden, with Lord Mountbatten memorabilia.

✉ 20 Monmouth Street, London WC2, ☎ 020 7836 4300, 📠 020 7240 3540, 🖰 resmon@radisson.com 🖵 www.radissonedwardian.com

Blooms Townhouse Hotel (Map D–C1)

Elegant 18th-century townhouse next to the British Museum; rooms have an English country house atmosphere.

✉ 7 Montague Street, WC1, ☎ 020 7323 1717, 📠 020 7636 6498, 🖰 blooms@grangehotels.com 🖵 www.bloomshotel.com

St Margaret's Hotel (Map D–C1)

Family-run hotel; 60 cheerful rooms (not all have en-suite facilities). Family rooms available.

✉ 26 Bedford Place, WC1, ☎ 020 7636 4277, 📠 (020) 7323 3066,

🖰 enquiries@stmargaretshotel.co.uk 🖵 www.stmargaretshotel.co.uk

• *BUDGET*

Ruskin (Map D–C1)

Excellent location in Bloomsbury, good value for money.

✉ 23–24 Montague Street, WC1, ☎ 020 7636 7388, 📠 020 7323 1662, 🖵 www.ruskinhotellondon.com

Ashlee House (Map C–F2)

Backpackers' hostel with rooms or dorms; clean, well-priced, and near the city centre.

✉ 261-5 Gray's Inn Road, WC1, ☎ 020 7833 9400, 📠 020 7833 9677, 🖰 info@ashleehouse.co.uk 🖵 www.ashleehouse.co.uk

Generator (Map C–F2)

Large hostel (837 beds), good facilities, reasonable prices, friendly staff. A great place to meet people.

✉ Compton Place, 37 Tavistock Place, WC1, ☎ 020 7388 7666, 📠

020 7388 7644, ☏ info
@the-generator.co.uk
🖳 www.
the-generator.co.uk

West and Southwest London

• **LUXURY**

Blakes (Map C–B6)
Popular with celebri-
ties. Glamorous
interiors and suites.
✉ 33 Roland Gardens,
London SW7, ☎ 020
7370 6701, ✆ 020 7373
0442, ☏ blakes@
blakeshotel.com
🖳 www.
blakeshotel.com

The Beaufort
(Map C–C5)
Stylish hotel with large,
modern rooms; very
good value for money.
✉ 33 Beaufort
Gardens, London SW3,
☎ 020 7584 5252,
✆ 020 7589 2834,
☏ reservations@
thebeaufort.co.uk
🖳 www.thebeaufort.
co.uk

**Knightsbridge
Hotel** (Map C–C5)
Handy for Harrods,
with opulent rooms;

full telecommunication
and other facilities.
✉ 10 Beaufort
Gardens, SW3,
☎ 020 7584 6300,
✆ 020 7584 6355,
☏ knightsbridge@
firmdale.com
🖳 www.firmdale.com

• **MID-RANGE**

The Gallery Hotel
(Map C–B5)
Traditional Georgian
hotel; spacious suites.
✉ 8–10 Queensberry
Place, London SW7,
☎ 020 7915 0000, ✆
020 7915 4400, ☏
thegallery@ eeh.co.uk
🖳 www.eeh.co.uk

The Pelham
(Map C–B5)
Small and comfort-
able; all the rooms are
individually decorated.
✉ 15 Cromwell Place,
London SW7, ☎ 020
7589 8288, ✆ 020 7584
8444, ☏ pelham
@firmdale.com
🖳 www.firmdale.com

Swiss House Hotel
(Map C–B6)
The rooms are good
value for the location,
near Hyde Park.

✉ 171 Old Brompton
Road, SW5, ☎ 020
7373 2769, ✆ 020 7373
4983, ☏ recep@
swiss-hh.demon.co.uk
🖳 www.
swiss-hh.demon.co.uk

• **BUDGET**

Amsterdam Hotel
(Map C–A6)
Comfortable B&B near
Earl's Court; all rooms
with en-suite facilities.
✉ 7 Trebovir Road,
London SW5, ☎ 020
7370 5084, ✆ 020 7244
7608, ☏ enquiries
@amsterdam-hotel.com
🖳 www.amsterdam-
hotel.com

Hotel 167 (Map C–B6)
Slightly upmarket
B&B; all the rooms
have en-suite facilities.
✉ 167 Old Brompton
Rd, SW5, ☎ 020 7373
3221, ✆ 020 7373
3360, ☏ enquiries@
Hotel167.com
🖳 www.hotel167.com

Victoria Hotel
(Map D–B6)
Recently refurbished,
great value, within
walking distance of
Westminster/Victoria.

✉ 71 Belgrave Rd, SW1, ☎ 020 7834 3077, ✆ 020 7932 0693, ✆ AstorVictoria @aol.com 💻 www. astorhostels.com

Rushmore Hotel

(Map C–A6)
Stylish; imaginative murals in bedrooms.
✉ 11 Trebovir Rd, SW5, ☎ 020 7370 3839, ✆ 020 7370 0274, ✆ rushmore-reservations@ london.com 💻 www. rushmorehotel.co.uk

Garden Court Hotel (Map C–A3)

Family-run hotel, very reasonably priced.
✉ 30-31 Kensington Gardens, SW2, ☎ 020 7229 2553, ✆ 020 7727 2749, ✆ info@ gardencourthotel.co.uk 💻 www. gardencourthotel.co.uk

The City, the East End and Docklands

• LUXURY

Great Eastern Hotel (Map C–H3)

Style guru Sir Terence Conran has made this one of the hippest hotels within strolling distance of the City.
✉ Liverpool St, EC2, ☎ 020 7618 5000, ✆ 020 7618 5001, ✆ reservations@ great-eastern-hotel. co.uk 💻 www.great-eastern-hotel.co.uk

The Rookery

(Map D–F1)
Discreet boutique hotel with 33 cosy rooms. Half-way between the City and the West End.
✉ Peter's Lane, Cowcross Street, EC1, ☎ 020 7336 0931, ✆ 020 7336 0932, ✆ reservations@ rookery.co.uk 💻 www. rookeryhotel.com

Four Seasons Canary Wharf

(Map E–A1)
This impeccable Docklands hotel is aimed squarely at the business market.
✉ Westferry Circus, Canary Wharf E14, ☎ 020 7510 1999, ✆ res.canarywharf@ fourseasons.com 💻 www.fourseasons. com/canarywharf

• MID-RANGE

Thistle City Barbican Hotel (Map C–G2)

Conveniently situated for the Barbican Arts Centre and the City.
✉ 120 Central Street, London EC1, ☎ 020 7251 1565, ✆ 0870 333 9201, ✆ CityBarbican@ Thistle.co.uk 💻 www. thistlehotels.com

Southwark Rose Hotel (Map C–G4)

Very attractive and stylish, small hotel; well priced, but rooms are on the small side.
✉ 43-47 Southwark Bridge Rd, SW1, ☎ 020 7015 1480, ✆ 020 7015 1481, ✆ info@southwark rosehotel.co.uk 💻 www.southwarkrose hotel.co.uk

• BUDGET

St Christopher's Inn (Map C–H4)

Well-run hostel with 164 beds, plus a roof garden with solarium and sauna. This inn is the flagship for this hostel chain.

✉ 163 Borough High Street, SE1, ☎ 020 7407 1856, 📠 020 7403 7715, 🖰 bookings @st-christophers.co.uk 🖥 www. st-christophers.co.uk

North London

• MID-RANGE
Hampstead Village Guest House
(Map F–B1)

Very characterful, with charming back garden (where you can have breakfast). Near Hampstead Heath, and 20 minutes by tube to the city centre.

✉ 2 Kemplay Rd, NW3, ☎ 020 7439 8679, 📠 020 7794 0254, 🖰 info@hamp-steadguesthouse.com 🖥 www.hampstead guesthouse.com

Camden Lock Hotel
(Map C–D1)

Modern hotel in trendy Camden Town overlooking the canal. Good transport links to the city centre.

✉ 89 Chalk Farm Road, NW1, ☎ 020 7267 3912, 📠 020

7267 5996, 🖰 info@ camdenlockhotel.co.uk 🖥 www.camdenlock hotel.co.uk

• BUDGET
St Chistopher's Inn
(Map C–E1)

The Camden branch of this hostel chain is small and friendly, although not in the quietest location.

✉ 48-50 Camden High Street, NW1, ☎ 020 7388 1012, 📠 020 7388 4200, 🖰 bookings@ st-christophers.co.uk 🖥 www. st-christophers.co.uk

Further Afield

• LUXURY
Petersham Hotel
(Map B–B3)

Classic, luxury hotel near Richmond Park, with lovely views over the Thames.

✉ Nightingale Lane, Richmond, Surrey, TW10 6UZ, ☎ 020 8940 7471, 📠 020 8939 1098, 🖰 enq@ petershamhotel.co.uk 🖥 www. petershamhotel.co.uk

• MID-RANGE
Riverside Hotel
(Map B–B3)

This is a family-run hotel located on the banks of the Thames with pleasant, reason-ably-priced rooms. Waterloo is just 20 minutes by train.

✉ 23 Petersham Road, Richmond, Surrey TW10 6UH, ☎ 020 8940 1339, 📠 020 8948 0967, 🖰 riversidehotel@ yahoo.com 🖥 www. riversiderichmond. co.uk

• BUDGET
Greenwich Parkhouse Hotel
(Map E–C5)

This small B&B has just eight rooms, but it has a great location on the very edge of Greenwich Park – from here you can catch a boat into town.

✉ 1 & 2 Nevada Street, Greenwich, SE10, ☎ 020 8305 1478, 🖰 b&b@ greenwich-parkhouse-hotel.co.uk 🖥 www. greenwich-parkhouse-hotel.co.uk

Afternoon Tea
Afternoon tea is a great British institution which shouldn't be missed. Mostly the speciality of the grand hotels, the set tea usually involves 'finger' sandwiches (cucumber, smoked salmon and the like) followed by assorted cakes, scones with cream, or pastries, served with a selection of teas. Most big hotels have dress codes (no jeans or trainers) and in some (such as the Ritz) advance bookings are required. Be prepared: it is about £30 a head.

EATING OUT

British food may once have been something of an international joke, epitomized by things like comforting, stodgy pies and puddings ('nursery food'), greasy fish and chips, and mammoth fry-ups for breakfast. But that is an image which is well past its sell-by date, particularly in London, where the range of cuisines available is huge and the variety of eateries (from pubs to trendy cafés, brasseries, wine bars, bistros and the like) has expanded enormously in recent years. Coupled with this, there has been a revolution in top-end gourmet restaurants where home-grown talent is now proving itself to be a match for the best anywhere else in the world. Whatever your budget or taste buds dictate, you can be sure that London will provide plenty of culinary adventures.

British Pubs

The most characteristic British drinking venue is, of course, the 'public house' or **pub**, a social institution which stretches back to the days of wayside coaching inns. London has a vast diversity of pubs, many of them dating from the Victorian era, and there are very few places where you

Left: *Hand-pumped beer is just one of the hallmarks of a typical traditional London pub.*
Opposite: *Tea at the Ritz is a British institution.*

won't find one within handy reach. Be warned though – they can be ghastly, with plastic decor, rude staff, terrible food and gassy beer (this is particularly true in the West End, where good pubs need some ferreting out). On the other hand, the best of them will feature a good range of 'real ales' (*see* panel, this page), a welcoming atmosphere, tasty snacks and an entertaining ambience. Many are still the centre of the surrounding communities, with 'locals' propping up the bar and socializing. Many more have also been refurbished and feature fringe theatre or cabaret performances, live music, and even their own on-site micro-breweries. Good food, too, has become much more important in recent years, and lunchtime is the most popular time to eat in a pub (if possible try to avoid the 13:00–14:00 crush when they're packed out with office workers).

Most pubs have a fairly limited selection of wine so, for that, you're better off heading for a **brasserie** or **wine bar**, of which there are scores throughout the capital.

Real Ales

The classic British pub drink is a pint of **bitter**, a dark, uncarbonated brew that comes in many guises. The best bitters are those pumped by hand from the cellar, and served at room temperature. In previous decades the big breweries swallowed up many traditional small brewers and imposed a uniformly bland, gassy product on many pubs: thanks to the efforts of CAMRA (the Campaign for Real Ale) this trend was halted (if not reversed), and to taste the real thing you should avoid pubs where the beer is served by electric pump. Chilled, draught **lager** and bottled lagers are also widely available in pubs, as is Guinness, a dark, creamy Irish **stout**. The main London breweries are Youngs and Fullers.

Right: *The City Barge at Strand-on-the-Green, Chiswick, is one of London's many historic pubs; it dates from 1484.*

Café Culture
Starbucks and other coffee chains are everywhere but if you're looking for a more traditional, individualistic coffee house then Soho is the place to go. Two old favourites are **Maison Bertaux** (⊠ 28 Greek St, W1) and **Patisserie Valerie** (⊠ 44 Old Compton Street, W1), both of which serve excellent pastries with their coffee. Beans from every coffee-growing country in the world are available at the aromatic **Monmouth Coffee Company** (⊠ 27 Monmouth St, WC2). For atmosphere alone it's also worth checking out the **Star Café** (⊠ 22 Great Chapel St, W1) and **Bar Italia** (⊠ 22 Frith St, W1).

Modern British Cuisine

A new wave of restaurateurs and chefs has added some spice and flair to British cuisine, proving that the capital is no longer the culinary backwater it was once thought to be – in fact, London now boasts more restaurants bearing the coveted Michelin star than any other European city, apart from Paris.

'New wave' British cuisine includes chefs such as Gordon Ramsey (Gordon Ramsey at Claridge's, Brook Street, W1), Matthew Harris (at Bibendum, Fulham Road, SW3), Fergus Henderson (at St John, in St John Street, EC1) and Mark Gregory (at Axis, Aldwych, WC2) who are all presently leading the way in top British cuisine. There is no overall style to this new wave, apart from a consistent sense of inventiveness and an eclectic use of ingredients and methods which draws on everything from West Coast/Californian to Mediterranean and Far Eastern influences.

Entertaining Themes

Another recent phenomenon on the London restaurant scene has been the rise of mega entertainment and eating venues, pioneered by style guru Sir Terence Conran with the opening of the massive 350-seat Quaglino's restaurant in 1994; in 1995 he followed this with the even bigger (700-seat) Mezzo, which is on two floors with glass-fronted kitchens, comprising two restaurants, a café and three bars. Meanwhile, Marco Pierre White has continued to expand his empire, which now includes the Mirabelle, the Criterion Brasserie and Quo Vadis, which is decorated with artworks by Damien Hirst. Planet Hollywood (backed by Hollywood heavies Sylvester Stallone, Bruce Willis and Arnold Schwarzenegger) in Piccadilly and the Sports Café in the Haymarket are all part of the same trend, while the Rainforest Café (situated in Shaftsbury Avenue) has a jungle theme – complete with lots of vegetation, a tropical fish tank and animatronic elephants, gorilla and (in the shop) even a crocodile.

Traditional British Food

Alongside the growth of 'modern British' cuisine (see page 62), there has also been a revival of traditional cooking in the capital's restaurants, with good, hearty food

---

Traditional Breakfasts
Traditional British breakfasts are quite legendary, and are usually served up to around 11:00 in hotels and cafés (some serve them all day). The obligatory fry-up of eggs, bacon, sausage and tomato is often supplemented by extras such as 'bubble and squeak', chips, baked beans, mushrooms, black pudding, kedgeree or kidneys. After one of these hearty breakfasts you'll be well set for a day's sightseeing.

Pubs and Live Bands
Pubs are a great place to watch live bands at (usually) low cost, but the quality varies widely. Some of the more promising venues include **Barfly** (✉ 49 Chalk Farm Rd, ☎ 020 7691 4244), the **Bull & Gate** (✉ 389 Kentish Town Rd, NW5, ☎ 020 7485 5358), the **Dublin Castle** (✉ 94 Parkway, Camden, ☎ 020 7485 1773), the **Hope & Anchor** (✉ 207 Upper Street, Islington N1, ☎ 020 7354 1312), and **Water Rats** (✉ 328 Gray's Inn Road, WC1, ☎ 020 7837 7269).

EATING OUT

Fish and Chips

Once considered to be the only worthwhile British culinary export to the world, fish and chips can be found almost everywhere – but standards vary widely. The best fish and chips are found in popular places such as the Sea Shell (in Lisson Grove) and Geale's (at Notting Hill Gate). There are also many excellent seafood restaurants where you can enjoy Dover sole, plaice, sea bass, or even Cockney staples such as cockles, or eel pie and mash.

The Small Print

In general, menu prices should include Value Added Tax (VAT) of 17.5%. Some restaurants will also impose a cover charge of £1–2 per head or have a minimum charge during busy periods. Most restaurants will add a service charge (usually between 10 and 15%) but be wary of those that then also leave the space for gratuities empty on your final bill, cheekily expecting you to add another 10%! It's amazing how many people fall for it – but remember, it's not a compulsory charge either way. If the service was bad, don't pay it.

thankfully banishing the excesses of nouvelle cuisine to the culinary dustbin. Some restaurants, of course, never followed fashion anyway, and places such as the 150-year-old Simpson's in the Strand, and the Quality Chop House (EC1), have been serving staples such as steak and kidney pudding and fish cakes since time immemorial. Dishes such as bangers and mash, meat casseroles and pies, shepherd's pie, toad-in-the-hole and roast beef with Yorkshire pudding are just some of the main courses you might come across. Desserts include treats such as jam roly-poly, trifles, toffee pudding, spotted dick and bread-and-butter pudding.

Ethnic Restaurants

London has always been known for its ethnic cuisine, in particular Indian, Bangladeshi and Chinese food. Many of the numerous curry houses tend to churn out identical dishes (with sauces bought in bulk) which have limited appeal, but to balance this there are many excellent establishments where freshly prepared ingredients are used to good effect in regional dishes from India, Nepal, Sri Lanka, Pakistan and Bangladesh.

A similar caveat applies to Chinese restaurants, in many of which monosodium glutamate (MSG) is heaped on regardless of all the health warnings: however, London also has some of the best Cantonese chefs in Europe (partly due to an exodus from Hong Kong before it reverted to Chinese rule in 1997), with *dim sum* (lunchtime snacks) one of the most characteristic features of the cuisine.

The range of ethnic restaurants does not stop there, however, and among the ones you may come across are Japanese, Korean, Thai, Malaysian, Indonesian, Turkish, Jewish, Vietnamese, Mongolian and various types of African and Caribbean. French, Italian and Greek are probably the most widespread of the European cuisines to be found here, but virtually all the others are also represented.

> **Ye Olde Cheshire Cheese**
> Situated at 15 Fleet Street (with its entrance in a side alley), this is one of the oldest inns in the city: parts of the labyrinthine premises date back to 1667. Past patrons include Samuel Pepys, Dr Johnson, Charles Dickens and Mark Twain.

Chain Restaurants

In addition to the ubiquitous fast-food places, London has several good-quality chains with reasonable prices and with branches in strategic locations. Look out for these: Café Rouge (French), Pret a Manger (chemical-free sandwiches and other snacks), Bella Pasta (Italian), Café Flo (French), Garfunkel's (American), Sofra (Turkish), Café Uno (Italian), Cork & Bottle (wine bars with good food), Micky's (mostly outside the city centre: proper traditional fish and chips at non-tourist prices).

Below: *Simpson's in the Strand is a good place to sample traditional roast beef and Yorkshire pudding.*

Cafés in galleries and museums should not be ignored: many are excellent. There's a detailed Eating Out listing in the weekly magazine *What's On*.

Above: *Shepherd Market is a popular spot for alfresco eating during the summer months.*

A Room With a View

As well as being a major arts centre, the **South Bank** has some excellent restaurants with views over the Thames and the city. Among the best are: **Le Pont de la Tour** (*see* page 69), the **Oxo Tower Restaurant and Brasserie** (✉ 8th Floor, Barge House, SE1, ☎ 020 7803 3888), the **People's Palace** (✉ Level 3, Royal Festival Hall, SE1, ☎ 020 7928 999), and the **Blue Print Café** (✉ Design Museum, Butler's Whaf, SE1, ☎ 020 7378 7031).

Whitehall and Westminster

Tate Britain Restaurant

This restaurant has a spacious, imposing setting, with a changing menu and excellent desserts.

✉ *Tate Britain, Millbank, London SW1,* ☎ *020 7887 8825.*

The Cinnamon Club

Indian food with a modern twist in old-fashioned, wood-panelled surroundings. Booking essential.

✉ *Old Westminster Library, Great Smith Street, SW1,* ☎ *020 7222 2555.*

The West End

Aperitivo

This restaurant specializes in the Italian equivalent of tapas.

✉ *41 Beak St, London W1,* ☎ *020 7287 2057.*

Tokyo Diner

Limited but excellent Japanese food at affordable prices.

✉ *2 Newport Place, London WC2,* ☎ *020 7287 8777.*

Gay Hussar

Famous and long-established Hungarian restaurant.

✉ *2 Greek Street, London W1,* ☎ *020 7437 0973.*

Hard Rock Café

Queues are one of the drawbacks of this famous burger joint decorated with rock memorabilia; prices are high but meals are usually worth the wait.
⊠ 150 Old Park Lane, London W1, ☎ 020 7629 0382.

Sports Café

Catch 150 satellite channels on 120 TV sets; restaurant, three bars and a dance floor.
⊠ 80 Haymarket, London SW1, ☎ 020 7839 8300.

The Stockpot

The food here is certainly not *haute cuisine*, but here is possibly the cheapest filling meal in town.
⊠ 38 Panton Street, London WC2, ☎ 020 7839 5142.

Kettners

Trendy pizza joint housed in interesting old building.
⊠ 29 Romilly Street, London W1, ☎ 020 7734 6112.

Sugar Club

This popular, two-storey restaurant has an innovative menu which focuses on Pacific Rim dishes. Booking in advance is essential.
⊠ 21 Warwick Street, W1, ☎ 020 7437 7776.

Bloomsbury and Covent Garden

Simpson's in the Strand

This is a very traditional restaurant – look out for waiters wheeling out silver platters of beef and the like. Serves excellent puddings and breakfasts.
⊠ 100 Strand, London WC2, ☎ 020 7836 9112.

Porters English Restaurant

Excellent traditional food is available at this restaurant, situated in the heart of Covent Garden.
⊠ 17 Henrietta Street, London WC2, ☎ 020 7836 6466.

Camden Pubs

Camden has a proliferation of good pubs, many of them with live music and most packed to overflowing at weekends. Some open only in the evenings. Among the more popular are **Oxford Arms** (a traditional pub with a beer garden and good bar food) and the **Fusilier and Firkin** (excellent locally brewed beers, good food and live music).

Booking Tables

You'll certainly need to book ahead for some of London's top eateries, and although not all restaurants insist on a reservation, it never does any harm. Getting a table at the more popular places is hardest from Thursday through to Saturday. A reliable internet booking service is 🖳 www.toptable.co.uk which also sometimes offers discounts. Many restaurants around Soho and the theatre areas are busiest before and after show times, so you stand a better chance of getting a table between 19:30 and 21:00.

Above: *Wagamama is a very popular Japanese eatery.*
Opposite: *A fashionable part of London, Covent Garden offers a wide choice of restaurants, cafés and wine bars.*

Family Feeding
Unlike their Continental counterparts, the Brits aren't renowned for welcoming kids into restaurants but they're getting more tolerant than they once were. There are plenty of fast food restaurants but for something a bit more classy you could try the **Hard Rock Café** (*see* page 67), **Rock Island Diner** (✉ 2nd floor, London Pavilion, Piccadilly Circus) or **Ed's Easy Diner** (✉ 12 Moor St, W1). Pizza chains such as **Pizza Express** are also a good bet.

Food for Thought
It's been here for 30 years and there are still queues at lunchtime: excellent vegetarian food at very reasonable prices.
✉ 31 Neal Street, WC2, ☎ 020 7836 9072.

Alastair Little
In the heart of Soho, there are always plenty of interesting choices on the daily changing set menu.
✉ 49 Frith St, W1, ☎ 020 7734 5183.

The Ivy
This oak-panelled restaurant is adored by celebrities, drawn by the star appeal of its modern European cooking.

✉ 1 West St, WC2, ☎ 020 7836 4751.

Wagamama
Very popular noodle bar chain: excellent for filling, tasty Japanese food in busy surroundings.
✉ 101A Wigmore Street, W1, ☎ 020 7409 0111.

West and Southwest London
Bibendum
Classy, eclectic cuisine is served here, in the delightful old Michelin building. Pricey, but worth it.
✉ Michelin House, 81 Fulham Rd, London SW3, ☎ 020 7581 5817.

Chutney Mary
Best of 'British Raj' cooking and regional Indian dishes.
✉ 535 King's Road, London SW10, ☎ 020 7351 3113.

La Gavroche
One of London's top restaurants, famous for the high standard

of its classic French cuisine.

✉ 43 Upper Brook Street, London W1, ☎ 020 7499 1826.

North London

Belgo Noord

A restaurant with amusing décor, and inexpensive, generous portions of Belgian favourites; but book in advance.

✉ 72 Chalk Farm Road, London NW1, ☎ 020 7267 0718.

Sea Shell

This is a top quality fish-and-chippie.

✉ 49–51 Lisson Grove, London NW1, ☎ 020 7224 9000.

Café Corfu

Excellent and wide-ranging menu of Greek specialities in this stylish restaurant.

✉ 7-9 Pratt Street, NW1 ☎ 020 7267 8088.

Jin Kichi

This small Japanese restaurant is a long-standing favourite for food grilled at your table, as well as classic sushi and sashimi.

✉ 73 Heath Street, Hampstead NW3, ☎ 020 7794 6158.

South and Southeast London

Butler's Wharf Chop House

Fabulous views of Tower Bridge from Terence Conran's riverfront restaurant. Traditional British food at its best.

✉ Butler's Wharf, 36E Shad Thames, London SE1, ☎ 020 7403 3403.

Le Pont de la Tour

Another Conran outpost, overlooking the river. Attentive service, exhaustive wine list, accent on seafoods.

✉ Butler's Wharf, 36D Shad Thames, London SE1, ☎ 020 7403 8403.

Bamboula

Get into the spirit of Brixton's Caribbean community with jerk chicken, rice'n'peas, curried goat and other ethnic dishes.

✉ 12 Acre Lane, Brixton, SW2, ☎ 020 7737 6633.

Above: *The skyline of the City of London, a mosaic of modern architecture, is very impressive at night.*

ENTERTAINMENT

The quality and variety of London's arts, culture and entertainment scene is probably unrivalled anywhere in the world. To navigate your way around this cultural maze, the most comprehensive listings of what's on are found in the weekly *Time Out*, and *What's On*, while the *Evening Standard* on Thursdays has an excellent listing supplement called *Metro Life*. Alternatively, call the 24-hour premium-rate information line: ☎ (09068) 663 344, and select the relevant menu options – have a pen and paper ready.

Nightlife

One of the city's most colourful areas, Soho buzzes with activity, particularly by night. Once London's principal red-light district, it has been cleaned up in recent years (although strip joints, including the famous Raymond Revuebar, still operate) and now offers a vast range of fashionable cafés, brasseries, restaurants, discos, clubs and, of course, cinemas and theatres.

Theatre

With a stage history that dates back to the father of theatre, William Shakespeare, it is

---

Theatre Tours
If you want to find out more about what goes on in some of London's famous theatres, you can take backstage tours (duration from 30 to 75 minutes) of several major theatres including the Royal National Theatre, South Bank Centre, ☎ (020) 7452 3400 (tours), 7452 3000 (box office); and the Theatre Royal, Drury Lane, Catherine St, WC2, ☎ (020) 7494 5000. A limited number of visitors can be accommodated on the tours, so it's sensible to book in advance.

little wonder that London is often seen as the theatre capital of the world. While the West End may appear to be dominated by blockbusting musicals, numerous other stages provide the platform for inventive, talented work and original productions. London is home to two great acting companies, the **Royal Shakespeare Company** and the **National Theatre**, but stars of the stage (and screen) can also be seen in productions away from the West End or mainstream theatres. There's also a thriving **fringe theatre** scene, with avant-garde plays staged in locations as diverse as pubs and converted warehouses. In any one week there may be around 200 shows on the go, so you will be spoilt for choice.

Music

London has a number of venues for classical music, ranging from the ornate splendour of the **Royal Albert Hall** to the three, purpose-built halls of the **South Bank Centre** (see page 47), the acoustically perfect **Wigmore Hall**, and the **Barbican Centre** complex, and on any one day there are likely to be several performances to choose from. The capital is home to the **Royal Philharmonic Orchestra**, the **London Symphony Orchestra**, the **London Philharmonic Orchestra**, the **Philharmonia**, and the **BBC Symphony Orchestra**, to name but the most prominent. Concerts are, in many cases, poorly attended (to the shame of the Londoners), so there is

---

Elizabethan Theatre
The 'golden age' of the Elizabethan era led to the flowering of literature and drama and the rise of playwrights and authors such as William Shakespeare, Ben Jonson and Christopher Marlowe. Theatre performances took place on temporary stages outside pubs, and were looked down upon by the city fathers as degenerate. James Burbage then constructed London's first theatre in Shoreditch, outside the City boundaries, in 1574. Later, he dismantled it to create the Globe in Southwark (see page 26), where Shakespeare's plays were first performed. The Globe has now been recreated, albeit not on the original site.

Below: *Modelled on a Roman amphitheatre, the Royal Albert Hall is one of the capital's largest concert halls.*

**London for Less and
the London Pass**
Whether tourist passes
save you money
depends on what you
plan to do, especially as
most museums and
galleries are now free
(see panel, page 73) –
but it is worth looking
at the possibilities.
Most families would
save with the **London
for Less card**: valid for
4 people for 8 days
with discounts of
10%–50% at 250
establishments of all
kinds, including some
major attractions. It is
available from tourist
information centres, or
☎ 0870 737 8080.
Keen sightseers might
benefit from **The
London Pass**, with free
admission to 60 sights
plus various discounts
over 1, 2, 3 or 6 days;
☎ (0870) 242 9988. It
includes a Travelcard if
pre-purchased through
the web 🖥 www.
londonpass.com

rarely a problem getting tickets. You can take advantage of free **lunchtime concerts** from Monday to Friday in many churches (such as St Martin-in-the-Fields, St James's Church in Piccadilly, and several others). Outdoor concerts are also held at **Kenwood House** in the summer; a wide range of works is also performed during the Henry Wood Promenade Concerts, '**The Proms**', (see panel, page 73) during summer.

Jazz is also easy to find, notably at Ronnie Scott's Club (one-night membership at the entrance). Booking advisable.

Opera

Built in the early 19th century, the **Royal Opera House** has recently reopened after major redevelopement. Opera was first staged here in 1817, and performances still pack the house despite exorbitant ticket prices. More reasonably priced performances can be seen at the **London Coliseum**, home to the **English National Opera**. New and innovative works are often performed during the summertime **Almeida Opera Festival** at the **Almeida Theatre** in Islington.

Dance

Dance in all its varied forms is well represented in the capital, with every style from the classic showpieces of the **Royal Ballet** to contemporary works and even Brazilian or Indian dance on display. Major venues include the **ICA**, the **London Coliseum**, the **Royal Opera House**, **Riverside Studios** (in Hammersmith), and the **South Bank Centre**. Touring companies often perform in London. See new talent at the annual **Dance Umbrella** festival in October/November.

Opposite: *Covent Garden is always alive with street entertainers and musicians playing all kinds of music.*

OPERA, DANCE & ART

Art

London offers not only some of the world's greatest collections of Western art but also a thriving contemporary scene with a huge range of new, creative talent on display. The historic collections that can be seen in the **National Gallery** (*see* page 16), **Tate Britain** (*see* page 35), **Tate Modern** (*see* page 18), **Courtauld Gallery** (*see* page 27), **British Museum** (*see* page 20) and **Victoria and Albert Museum** (*see* page 23) provide riches to sustain the enthusiast.

In modern art, the work of dynamic young artists (names to look for include Damien Hirst, Helen Chadwick, Mat Collishaw, Fiona Rae and Anya Gallacio, among others) can often be seen – for free – in the **commercial galleries** of Dering and Cork streets, both in the West End. The **Summer Exhibition** at the Royal Academy mostly features amateur artists, but the **Turner Prize** exhibits, on display at Tate Britain in November, are worth seeing. Summer **degree shows** are held at London art colleges in late May/June, in particular those at Goldsmiths, the Royal College, the Royal Academy, the Slade, and St Martin's School of Art.

Free Culture
London is expensive, but most major museums and galleries are now free – if this is to continue, voluntary contributions are essential, so please put something in the boxes if you can. Among the most popular freebies are the groups at South Kensington and Greenwich, the British Museum, National Gallery, National Portrait Gallery, both Tates, Imperial War Museum, Museum of London, Museum of Garden History, Photographers Gallery, Wallace Collection, Kenwood House and Sir John Soane's Museum.

The Promenade Concerts
From July to September each year the Royal Albert Hall hosts a series of virtuoso classical performances under the umbrella of the **Henry Wood Promenade Concerts** (usually known as 'the Proms'). The atmosphere is particularly lively on the famous Last Night of the Proms. Apply in writing for tickets, using *BBC Proms Guide*, available from bookshops and newsagents.

Getting Tickets
Buy tickets from the
venue if possible, since
you'll save on commis-
sion charges. If the
venue has sold out you
can often get them
through agencies like
Ticketmaster, ☎ 0870
534 4444, 🖳 www.
ticketmaster.co.uk;
Stargreen ☎ (020)
7734 8932, 🖳 www.
stargreen.co.uk; or
Ticketweb ☎ 08700
600 100, 🖳 www.
ticketweb.co.uk. Avoid
buying from the touts
outside venues – the
ticket may well be fake.

Half-price Theatre
On the south side of
Leicester Square, the
Society of West End
Theatres operates **tkts**
(a **ticket booth** where
you can get seats for
the day's performance
at half-price +£2.50 for
most West End shows).
🕐 10:00–19:00 Mon–
Sat, 12:00–15:00 Sun.
Tickets are never avail-
able for sell-out shows,
but they can some-
times be bought in
advance from official
booking agencies such
as Ticketmaster,
☎ 0870 534 4444,
🖳 www.ticketmaster.
co.uk, if you are pre-
pared to pay hefty
booking fees. Buying
tickets from touts out-
side theatres is not
advisable.

Festivals

If you're in the city for the **Chinese New Year** (late Jan or early Feb) head down to **Gerrard Street** to witness one of the noisiest celebrations in the capital, with firecrackers exploding all over the place as colourful papier-mâché lions dance through Chinatown trying to grab the cabbages, decorated with bank notes, which residents hang from their windows. This exuberant event attracts Chinese people, as well as sightseers, from all over London.

From Saturday through to Monday on the August Bank Holiday weekend every year, the **Notting Hill** area heaves with hundreds of thousands of people celebrating the famous **Carnival** – ear-splitting reggae, Caribbean soca, hip-hop and other music booms out from dozens of sound systems set up in the streets. The main events are the costume parades on Sunday and Monday, and the steel band contest on Saturday, with massive, colourful floats and extraordinarily ornate costumes. There are also several stages for live music, and stalls everywhere selling Red Stripe, Jamaican patties and other exotica.

Festivals & Spectator Sports

Several **ceremonies** take place at the Tower of London (*see page 19*). The 700-year-old traditional **Ceremony of the Keys** takes place nightly at 21:53, as the Chief Yeoman Warder locks the Tower gates and performs a ritual exchange which has remained unchanged since the reign of Queen Elizabeth I. For tickets to witness this ancient ceremony, write at least two months in advance to ✉ Ceremony of the Keys, HM Tower of London, London EC3N 4AB. Enclose a self-addressed envelope or international reply coupon and the names and addresses of all the members of the group for which you want to book (specify the age of under-18s and be sure to give three alternative dates).

Royal Gun Salutes mark royal birthdays and other state occasions. The medieval **Beating of the Bounds**, defining the parish boundaries, takes place at the Tower every three years on Ascension Day.

> ### Beefeaters and Ravens
> The Tower of London was the city's first zoo, with leopards, elephants, birds and polar bears on display in medieval times. In the 19th century this menagerie was transferred to London Zoo, but the ravens – feeding on scraps from the palace kitchens and, it is said, pecking away at severed heads from executions – stayed on. An old legend has it that 'only so long as they stay will the White Tower stand' and since Charles II's time they have been protected by royal decree.

Spectator Sports

There are numerous opportunities to participate in sporting activities in and around London. Many top international fixtures take place in the hallowed grounds of sporting venues such as **Lord's** (cricket), **Wimbledon** (tennis), **Crystal Palace** (athletics), **Wembley Stadium** (football), and **Twickenham** (Rugby Union). In addition, world-famous horse races take place at locations such as **Ascot**, **Epsom**, and **Sandown Park**. For more information about sporting events and venues, see pages 41–42.

Opposite: *Chinese New Year is a joyous celebration, when Chinatown comes alive with parades.*
Below: *Beefeaters have been guarding the Tower since the time of Henry VIII.*

Above: *Ronnie Scott's, where the best jazz can be heard, has been around for ages.*

Nightclubs

Once the pubs have shut, Londoners go clubbing – well into the small hours. The city has always prided itself on being at the cutting edge of dance culture. The club scene changes fast, so check listings magazines such as *Time Out* for the latest.

Bar Rumba

An old favourite, this small club always has great dance music. ✉ *36 Shaftesbury Avenue W1*, ☎ *(020) 7287 6933,* 🖥 *www. barrumba.co.uk*

The Cross

Tucked away beneath the King's Cross railway arches, this more-than-hip venue is famed for its funky house nights as well as mixed/gay Fridays. ✉ *27-31 King's Cross Goods Yard, N1,* ☎ *(020) 7837 0828,* 🖥 *www.the-cross.co.uk*

The Fridge

One of the longest-running venues, still massively popular with everyone from dreadlocked locals to techno ravers dancing to a variety of club nights and live bands. ✉ *1 Town Hall Parade, Brixton, SW2,* ☎ *(020) 7326 5100,* 🖥 *www.fridge.co.uk*

Heaven

London's biggest and best-known gay nightclub, although they also have mixed nights. ✉ *Under the Arches, Villiers Street, WC2,* ☎ *(020) 7930 2020,* 🖥 *www.heaven-london.com*

Ministry of Sound

A giant among clubs, now a global brand; popular for all-night dancing to big-name international DJs.

NIGHTCLUBS & LIVE MUSIC

✉ *103 Gaunt Street, SE1,* ☎ *(020) 7740 8600,* 🖥 *www.ministryofsound.com*

Pacha London

London outpost of the seminal Ibiza club, with fabulous décor; brings out the bling-bling in glamorous clubbers movin' to hip-hop, soul and boogie beats. ✉ *Terminus Place, Victoria, SW1,* ☎ *(020) 7833 3139,* 🖥 *www.pachalondon.com*

Live Music

London is a great city for live music. As well as being a stop for major artists on an international tour, there are also many up-and-coming local bands worth catching.

Carling Academy Brixton

One of London's biggest and best venues; its sloping floor means everyone gets a good eyeful. ✉ *211 Stockwell Rd, Brixton, SW9,* ☎ *(020) 7771 3000,* 🖥 *www.brixton-academy.co.uk*

Forum

Formerly the famous Town and Country Club, this is a great venue to catch soon-to-be-famous talents. ✉ *9-17 Highgate Rd, Kentish Town, NW5,* ☎ *(020) 7284 1001,* 🖥 *www.meanfiddler.com*

100 Club

This renowned venue has seen everyone from Glenn Miller to the Stones tread its boards. ✉ *100 Oxford Street, W1,* ☎ *(020) 7636 0933,* 🖥 *www.the100club.co.uk*

Ronnie Scott's

One of the world's famous jazz clubs, still going strong. ✉ *47 Frith Street, W1,* ☎ *(020) 7439 0747,* 🖥 *www.ronniescotts.co.uk*

Africa Centre

Top African bands play at this venue most Friday nights. ✉ *38 King Street, WC2,* ☎ *(020) 7836 1973,* 🖥 *www.africacentre.org.uk*

Pizza Express Jazz Club

Contemporary jazz is played to a respectful audience in this well-known basement venue below the pizza restaurant. ✉ *10 Dean Street, Soho, W1,* ☎ *(020) 7439 8722,* 🖥 *www.pizzaexpress.co.uk*

Spitz

This establishment, a combination of restaurant, café and music venue, hosts some interesting acts, with everything from jazz fusion to Icelandic singers. ✉ *Old Spitalfields Market, 109 Commercial Street, EC1,* ☎ *(020) 7392 9032,* 🖥 *www.spitz.co.uk*

Underworld

Located beneath the World's End pub, this maze of corridors and bars has everything from indie to rock bands. ✉ *174 Camden High Street, NW1,* ☎ *(020) 7482 1932.*

Above: *Canterbury's stately cathedral.*
Opposite: *The Royal Pavilion in Brighton.*

EXCURSIONS

Many interesting places are within easy reach of the capital. With frequent train services from the eight main rail termini in central London you don't have to worry about driving either; there are several coach services from Victoria Coach Station daily.

Canterbury has long been a place of pilgrimage, with the focal point being the city's magnificent cathedral. **Brighton**, with its Regency heritage, has great shopping and a traditional seaside pier; the highlight is the refurbished Royal Pavilion, the seaside palace of George IV.

The coast of Central Southern England features numerous popular seaside resorts and the historic naval port of **Portsmouth**. Inland are the ancient cathedral cities of **Winchester** and **Salisbury**. Near Salisbury, the monoliths of **Stonehenge** are one of England's best-known prehistoric monuments.

In Avon county, **Bath** was first popularized by the Romans as a spa town and with its fine Georgian architecture is one of the country's most elegant towns (with good shops, too). North of Bath, the **Cotswolds** are famous for their pretty, honey-coloured sandstone villages set among rolling hills.

One of the finest medieval castles is in the northwest at **Warwick**, while **Stratford-upon-Avon** is the birthplace of Shakespeare.

In Central England is **Oxford**, where many graceful college buildings are open to the public. Further east, the rival university town of **Cambridge** also boasts many fine buildings which can be explored by punt along the river or on foot.

Victoria Coach Station
✉ 164 Buckingham Palace Road, SW1
☎ (020) 7730 3466

The following tour operators offer day-tours from London to all the major tourist destinations, and all use qualified Blue Badge Guides:

Golden Tours
☎ (020) 7233 7030

Evan Evans
☎ (020) 7950 1777

Frames Rickards
☎ (020) 7828 9720

Hallam Anderson Tours
☎ (020) 7436 9304

Canterbury and Brighton

One of the oldest centres of Christianity in Britain, Canterbury is dominated by its magnificent **cathedral**. The narrow, winding streets around it can get overcrowded in summer but the cathedral itself is well worth the journey. Home to the country's most famous martyr – archbishop Thomas a Becket, who was murdered in 1170 – the cathedral became the focus of medieval pilgrimages which were immortalized in Geoffrey Chaucer's *Canterbury Tales*. Inside, notable features include the spot where Becket was killed (marked by a plaque), the 12th-century stained-glass windows, the beautiful fan vaulting of the Bell Harry Tower, and the tombs of Henry IV and the Black Prince.

At the **Canterbury Tales**, a series of waxwork tableaux recreate the experiences of 14th-century pilgrims. The new **Museum of Canterbury** has a range of displays from pre-Roman times to the present, many with interactive features designed to appeal to families. The pedestrianized city centre has plenty of good shops and restaurants.

Brighton is a heady mixture of seaside sauciness, sophisticated culture, intriguing shops, and excellent cafés and restaurants. Take a turn on the gaudy **Palace Pier**, and visit the **Royal Pavilion**, an outrageous blend of Indian, Chinese and Islamic architecture. The best pubs, restaurants, antique shops and fashion boutiques are found in a maze of narrow streets near the seafront known as the **Lanes**.

Canterbury
Location: Map G–C4
Distance from London: 90km (56 miles)
Tourist information:
☎ 01227 378100; 🖥 www.canterbury.co.uk
Cathedral: ☎ 01227 762862; 🖥 www.canterbury-cathedral.org.uk; ⏰ weekdays 09:00–18:00 (summer), 09:00–16:30 (winter), Sun 09:00–14:00, 16:30–17:30.
Canterbury Tales: ☎ 01227 454888; 🖥 www.canterburytales.org.uk; ⏰ 10:00–16:30 (winter); 09:30–17:00 (summer).
Museum of Canterbury: ☎ 01227 475 202; 🖥 www.canterbury-museum.co.uk; ⏰ 10:30–17:00 (last admission 16:00) Mon–Sat, Jun–Sep 13:30–17:00 Sun (last admission 16:00).

Brighton
Location: Map G–B4
Distance from London: 82km (51 miles)
Tourist Information:
☎ 0906 711 2255; 🖥 www.visitbrighton.com

Salisbury
Location: Map G–B4
Distance from London:
140km (87 miles)
Tourist Information:
☎ 01722 334956;
🖥 www.visitsalisburyuk.
com
Cathedral: ☎ 01722
555120; 🖥 www.
salisburycathedral.co.uk
🕓 07:15 daily, closes
18:15 Sep–May and
Sun all year; 19:15
Jun–Aug.
The Medieval Hall:
☎ 01722 412472;
🖥 www.medieval-hall.
co.uk; 🕓 11:00–17:00
Apr–Sep.
**Salisbury and South
Wiltshire Museum:**
☎ 01722 332151; 🖥
www.salisburymuseum.
org.uk; 🕓 Mon–Sat
10:00–17:00 all year;
14:00–17:00 Sun
Jul–Aug.

Stonehenge
Tourist Information:
☎ 01980 624715; 🖥
www.english-heritage.
org.uk/stonehenge
🕓 daily 09:30–16:00
(winter), 09:30–18:00
(summer).

Salisbury and Stonehenge

Salisbury has probably the finest medieval **cathedral** in Britain – completed in the 13th century, it displays a much greater unity of style than many others. Its most prominent feature is the elegant spire, at 123m (404ft) the tallest in Britain. Inside you can see Britain's oldest working clock (AD1386), a unique 13th-century frieze of bible stories in the Chapterhouse, and one of four original copies of the Magna Carta. Angelic-looking choristers sing at daily services, extending an 800-year tradition of worship.

Within the cathedral close is a magnificent 13th-century banqueting hall known as the **Medieval Hall**. In this venerable setting an audiovisual show, Discover Salisbury, covers the city past and present. Displays on the Neolithic history of Wessex and other aspects of the region are part of the wonderful collections at the award-winning **Salisbury and South Wiltshire Museum**, opposite the main portal of the cathedral.

Some 14km (10 miles) north of Salisbury is **Stonehenge**, an impressive monument to Neolithic civilization. Surrounded by the remains of ceremonial structures (some of them even older than Stonehenge itself), it is an awe-inspiring testament to the construction skills of early man. One of its most remarkable features is the stones' alignment with the rising and setting sun, but its exact role as a place of sun worship or as an astrological observatory is still a mystery.

Bath and the Cotswolds

The elegant town of Bath is an ancient Roman spa which was revived by fashionable society in the 18th century. A good starting point is **Abbey Church Yard**, a focal point of the city where street entertainers perform regularly. On the south side is **Bath Abbey**, built on the site of a Saxon church where King Edgar was crowned in AD973. It's a beautiful building, renowned for its lofty choir vault and lovely stained glass.

Bath's top attraction is the **Roman Baths and Museum**. Allow at least an hour to visit this complex; the tour encompasses the architectural remains of the Temple of Sulis Minerva, the Temple Courtyard, and the King's Bath, built around the city's hot spring and the heart of the Roman and Georgian spas. Afterwards, take a break in the 18th-century **Pump Room**, and have tea or lunch in surroundings much loved by Bath's most famous literary scion, Jane Austen.

Bath's famous Georgian terraces – the well-proportioned **Royal Crescent** and the equally harmonious **Circus** – are Britain's best examples of Regency architecture.

To the north of Bath lie the **Cotswolds**, a picturesque area well-known for its quaint, sleepy villages and gently rolling hills ('wolds'). The much-photographed villages owe their architectural uniformity to the use of the local limestone, which gives everything a honey-coloured hue. This is typically English countryside, with church steeples rising above fields enclosed by dry-stone walls where sheep and cattle graze.

Above: *Bath Abbey looms over the Roman Baths.*
Opposite: *Ancient Stonehenge at dusk.*

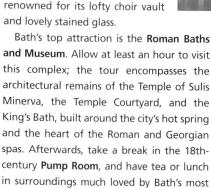

Bath
Location: Map G–B4
Distance from London: 187km (116 miles)
Tourist Information: ☎ 0906 7112000; 🖳 www.visitbath.co.uk
Bath Abbey: ☎ 01225 422462; ◷ daily 09:00–1800 (summer), 09:00–16:30 (winter).
Roman Baths and Museum: ☎ 01225 477785; 🖳 www. romanbaths.co.uk; ◷ daily 09:30–16:30 (winter), 09:00–17:00 (spring, autumn), 09:00–21:00 (Jul–Aug).

The Cotswolds
Tourist Information: ☎ 01452 425673; 🖳 www.the-cotswolds.org

Above: *Shake-speare's Birthplace, the big attraction in Stratford-upon-Avon.*

<u>Stratford-upon-Avon</u>
Location: Map G–B3
Distance from London: 137km (85 miles)

Tourist Information:
☎ 01789 293127;
💻 www.shakespeare-country.co.uk
All Shakespeare properties can be visited on a 'multiple house ticket';
☎ 01789 204016;
💻 www.shakespeare.org.uk ⏰ Jan–Mar daily 11:00–16:00; Apr–May daily 11:00–17:00; Jun–Aug Mon–Sat 09:30–17:00, Sun 10:00–17:00; Sep–Oct daily 11:00–17:00; Nov–Dec Mon–Sat 11:00–16:00, Sun 12:00–16:00.

Warwick Castle:
☎ 0870 442 2000;
💻 www.warwick-castle.co.uk
⏰ daily 10:00–17:00 (winter), 10:00–18:00 (summer).

Stratford-upon-Avon and Warwick Castle

This busy town on the River Avon makes the most of its association with William Shakespeare, who was born here on April 23, 1564. Foremost among its attractions is **Shakespeare's Birthplace**, a half-timbered building which is entered via The Shakespeare Exhibition; the latter provides a good introduction to his life and background while the former is an evocative re-creation of Tudor life when Will was a child. Also in the Old Town is **Hall's Croft**, an impressive 16th-century house owned by Shakespeare's son-in-law, Dr John Hall. On Chapel Street you'll find Nash's House and New Place, where Shakespeare spent his retirement years.

Outside of town is the famous **Anne Hathaway's Cottage**, the thatched and picturesque home of Shakespeare's wife. It still contains the Hathaway bed and many other items owned by the family, and has a gorgeous cottage garden. Another place of pilgrimage is the **Holy Trinity Church**, where Shakespeare is buried.

Eight miles to the northeast of Stratford is the well-preserved **Warwick Castle**, which is over a thousand years old. Now owned by the Tussaud's Group, it offers a number of interactive experiences including 'Ghosts Alive' in the 14th-century Ghost Tower, and 'Death or Glory' in the Armoury. Other attractions include the Great Hall, battlements, dungeons, state rooms, and 24ha (60 acres) of grounds.

Oxford and Cambridge

The university town of **Oxford** has its origins in the 12th century when students first clustered around the learned monasteries on the banks of the River Cherwell, thus creating Britain's first university town. The collegiate system developed during the 16th century; the city now has 36 colleges, with a student population of around 17,000.

Oxford's mix of students, tourists and residents keeps it lively – yet it still manages to retain something of 'that sweet city with her dreaming spires' beloved of poets and scholars. A central landmark is the **Carfax Tower**, the only surviving remnant of a 14th-century church, from the top of which (99 steps) there is an excellent view of the city.

Some of the ancient colleges are open to the public for a small charge, though they may be closed during exams (May–Jun). One of the loveliest is **Magdalen College** (pronounced *maud-len*), but others worth seeing are Merton, Corpus Christi, Trinity and Balliol. In summer, punting on the **River Cherwell** is an agreeable way to see the riverside façades of the colleges.

Traditionally a rival to Oxford, **Cambridge** was founded slightly later. It tends to be quieter and more peaceful than Oxford, and its pedestrianized city centre means that it's a pleasure to explore on foot. The city centre lies across a bend in the River Cam with the most picturesque section, known as the **Backs**, affording great views of six of the most central colleges. This is an excellent place for picnics and punting.

Oxford
Location: Map G–B3
Distance from London: 90km (56 miles)
Tourist Information:
☎ 01865 249811;
🖥 www.visitoxford.org
Carfax Tower:
✉ Queen & Cornmarket Streets, ☎ 01865 792653; ⏰ 10:00–17:30 Apr–Oct, 10:00–15:30 Nov–Mar.

Cambridge
Location: Map G–C3
Distance from London: 97km (60 miles)
Tourist Information:
☎ 01223 322640;
🖥 www.visitcambridge.org

Below: *Punting on the River Cam in Cambridge.*

Above: *London's black cabs now come in many different colours.*

Disabled Travellers
Artsline (free information on access to all arts and entertainment venues and events),
☎ (020) 7388 2227.
Holiday Care Service (an advisory service on accessible attractions and accommodation for the disabled),
☎ 0845 124 9971,
🖳 www.holidaycare. org.uk
Tripscope (information on transport for the disabled and elderly),
☎ 0845 758 5641.

Tourist Information

Overseas offices of the **British Tourist Authority** (BTA) have a range of leaflets, brochures, free maps and guides, and events calendars. Offices can be found in Australia (Sydney), Canada (Mississauga), Ireland (Dublin), New Zealand (Auckland), South Africa (Johannesburg), Singapore, and the USA (New York City); or you can visit their website at 🖳 www. visitbritain.com

The main tourist office in London is the **British Visitor Centre**, ✉ 1 Lower Regent Street, SW1, 🕑 Mon 09:30–18:30, Tue–Fri 09:00–18:30 and Sun 10:00–16:00 all year; Sat 09:00–17:00 June–Oct, 10:00–16:00 Nov–May. The centre does not accept telephone calls, but does have an information website, 🖳 www. visitlondon.com

TIC (tourist information centre) desks are located at **Heathrow Airport** tube stations in Terminals 1, 2 and 3, 🕑 daily 08:00–18:00 (to 19:00 Jun–Sep); **Liverpool Street Station** tube, 🕑 Mon–Fri 08:00–17:30, Sat 09:00–17:30; and **Waterloo Eurostar Terminal**, 🕑 daily 08:30–22:30. Several local TICs provide comprehensive information about their immediate areas, notably: in the City, Southwark and Greenwich.

Entry Requirements

No visas are required by citizens of the United States, Canada, Japan, Australia, New Zealand, Austria, Iceland, Finland, Switzerland and the European Union (EU). Many other Commonwealth citizens are also exempt, but should nevertheless check beforehand, as should nationals of all other countries.

Customs

For goods bought outside the EU, these restrictions on tax- and duty-free goods apply:

• 200 cigarettes, or 100 cigarillos, or 50 cigars, or 250g (8 ounces) tobacco.

• 2 litres (4 pints) still table wine plus 1 litre (2 pints) spirits or liqueur (over 22% proof), or 2 litres (4 pints) of fortified or sparkling wine (under 22% proof).

• 60ml (2 fluid ounces) perfume plus 250ml (8 fluid ounces) of toilet water.

• Other goods valued to £145.

Restrictions apply on the import of other items (firearms, protected species, meat products, etc.) and pets. There are no restrictions on currency.

Health Requirements

No vaccinations are required.

Money Matters

Currency: British currency is the pound sterling (£), divided into 100 pence (p). Coin denominations are 1p, 2p, 5p, 10p, 20p, 50p, £1 and £2. Notes are in denominations of £5, £10, £20, £50.

Banks: The four major banks, with branches throughout the city, are: Barclays, National Westminster, Lloyds and HSBC. Standard opening hours are ☺ 09:30–17:00, Mon–Fri, but there are variations. Some branches open for a few hours on Sat.

Currency Exchange: Traveller's cheques: You'll need your passport when cashing traveller's cheques. Commission is usually charged. Banks offer the best rates, but the numerous **bureaux de change** work longer hours.

Credit cards: Most hotels, shops and restaurants accept international credit cards.

VAT: Consumer goods (with major exceptions such as food and books) are subject to a 17.5% sales tax known as VAT (Value Added Tax). Visitors from non-EU countries can recoup VAT on major items but, before you buy, ask for the appropriate form. Customs will validate this when you leave.

Tipping: Service charges are usually included in bills, but many restaurants leave a blank space on credit card counterfoils to encourage customers to tip twice! If a tip is not included in the bill, waiters expect around 10–15%. Hairdressers and taxis expect a tip of about 10%. If there's a saucer in well-maintained washrooms, feel free to add a coin or two. Don't tip at all if the service has been really poor. Bar staff (but not in pubs) may also expect a tip.

Accommodation

London has many options, ranging from the **deluxe** to homely **bed and breakfasts** (B&Bs), **hostels** and **budget hotels**. Even in peak season there is rarely a shortage of places to stay, but nevertheless bear in mind that London is an expensive city, and this is more than reflected in the price of hotel rooms.

Accommodation agencies:

Super Breaks can offer discounts on over 100 hotels in the London area;
☎ (020) 7932 2020.
🕐 08:00–23:00.

British Hotels Reservation Centres (BHRC) have branches at Heathrow, Gatwick and City airports, Victoria, Paddington and Waterloo rail stations and Victoria coach station. Bookings are free;
☎ (020) 7340 1616;
🖥 www.bhrconline.com

Hotels and B&Bs: Hotels are classified by stars and all other types of accommodation by diamonds (both 1–5), with ratings depending on quality and range of facilities. These determine categories but give no indication of character or style. Establishments with four or more rooms are required to display notices of the charges, and whether these include breakfast, service charges, VAT, etc. In the off-peak winter season, you could negotiate a discount if you're staying for several days, but bargaining is not the norm. Many

of the upmarket hotels offer special weekend rates to fill rooms usually occupied by weekday business guests, so look into these mini-packages if you want to treat yourself to a weekend in a smart hotel. Most of the top London hotels are centred around Knightsbridge, Mayfair and Belgravia. A double room in the famous Dorchester Hotel or Claridges will cost in excess of £300 per night, but with a level of service commensurate with the high price. International chain hotels catering for business clients – such as the Hilton, Inter-Continental and Marriott – are in a similar bracket.

Hostels: There'a a good choice of hostels, most charging £20 or so per person, including several members of the YHA;
☎ (020) 7236 4965;
🖥 www.yha.org.uk

Bed and Breakfasts are a relative bargain in price terms; ask the tourist office or use an agency. Some are: the **London Bed & Breakfast Agency**, ☎ (020) 7586 2768, 🖳 www.londonbb.com **London Homestead Services**, ☎ (020) 8949 4455, 🖳 www.lhslondon.com **At Home in London**, ☎ (020) 8748 1943, 🖳 www.athomeinlondon.co.uk **Self-catering apartments** can offer good value for families, starting at about £250 a week (up to ten times that!).

Eating Out

London restaurants cater to every taste and budget – the diversity is almost unmatched by any other capital city. Even traditional **British cooking**, once a by-word for stodgy food, has been revitalized by a new generation of chefs and can now hold its own against the classic cuisines. **French**, **Italian** and **Greek** restaurants are all very common, while virtually every other European cuisine, from Spanish to Swedish, is easy to find. Britain has long been known for its ethnic foods, particularly **Chinese** and **Indian**; **Turkish**, **Thai**, **Malaysian**, **Lebanese** and **Japanese** restaurants are numerous and most other national cuisines are represented.

In recent years **pub food** has improved enormously, and while it may be hard to find a freshly made sandwich in some areas, in others the range and quality of bar food is as good as some restaurants. There are also a number of **bistros** and **wine bars**, where as well as sampling a range of fine wines you can find salads, light meals, and other fare. If all else fails, a **café** or **tearoom** can

Useful Contacts
Travel information with service updates, plus enquiry service for the underground and buses, ☎ (020) 7222 1234 (24 hours a day, 7 days a week).
National train enquiries, ☎ 08457 48 49 50.
National Express (coach service), ☎ 08705 80 80 80.
Heathrow airport, ☎ 0870 000 0123.
Gatwick airport, ☎ 0870 000 2468.
London City airport, ☎ (020) 7646 0000.
Stansted airport, ☎ 0870 000 0303.
Airbus service (to Heathrow), ☎ 0807 574 7777.
Victoria Coach station, ☎ (020) 7730 3466.
Docklands Light Railway, ☎ (020) 7363 9700.
Public Carriage Office (complaints), for black cabs: ☎ (020) 7941 7800.
Radio Taxis, ☎ (020) 7272 0272.
Dial-a-Cab, ☎ (020) 7253 5000.
Car Rental, Avis: ☎ 0870 606 0100; Hertz: ☎ 0870 599 6699; Budget: ☎ 0800 181 181.

Good Reading
• Duncan, Andrew (1995) *Secret London*. New Holland, London. Explores little-known and hidden facets of the capital, with 20 miles of walks.
• Duncan, Andrew (1991) *Walking London*. New Holland, London. Features 30 original walks in and around the capital.
• Porter, Roy. *London: A Social History*. Hamish Hamilton. Engaging and comprehensive account of the capital's development.
• Tames, Richard (1992) *Traveller's History of London*. Windrush Press. A lively and compact account of the capital's history, from Londinium to Docklands.
• Hamilton, Patrick. *20,000 Streets Under the Sky*. Hogarth/Trafalgar. Romantic trilogy set in the sleazy Soho of the 1930s.

usually provide tasty snacks, sandwiches or a quick meal.

Transport

London Underground and London Buses operate a 24-hour telephone service for travel information, ☎ (020) 7222 1234.

Travel Information Centres can provide useful free leaflets and pocket maps on bus and tube services; they are located at Oxford Circus, Piccadilly Circus, Hammersmith and St James's Park tube stations and at Euston, Paddington, King's Cross and Liverpool Street mainline stations, as well as in all four terminals at Heathrow Airport. If you're planning on using public transport extensively during the course of a day it's worth investing in a **Travelcard**, valid during off-peak times only (from 09:30 weekdays, all day at weekends) but good value compared to individual tickets (a one-day travelcard is £5.10 for two zones, which compares to single-journey tube tickets of £1.60 in zone 1, £2.00 for zones 1 & 2, and £3.70 for all zones). Travelcards can be used on tubes, most buses and Docklands Light Railway. There are also weekly travelcards (for which a photo is required) and carnets: books of 10 tube tickets. Buses are cheaper than tubes, a fact reflected in the cost of bus passes: £2 (1 day) or £8.50 (7 days), compared with a flat rate of £1 per bus in the centre. Airbuses and tube/DLR travel before 09:30 are excluded from passes and travelcards.

Business Hours

Most **shops** are open ⏰ 09:30–17:30, Mon–Sat, although different areas have their own late-night shopping days (Wednesday in

Knightsbridge, Thursday in Oxford Street, etc). Large supermarket chains stay open very late (some for 24 hours) Mon–Sat, and small corner shops (similar to convenience stores) stay open until 22:00 or later. Sunday trading is now firmly established in London, with supermarkets and many of the department stores open ⊕ 12:00–16:00.

Office hours are usually ⊕ 09:30–17:30, Mon–Fri (for **banks** see under Money Matters, p. 85). Office workers usually have a lunch hour between noon and 14:00. Opening hours of **museums** and **tourist attractions** vary enormously, but most are open daily by ⊕ 10:00 and close somewhere between 17:30 and 18:30, with shorter hours on Sundays. Virtually everything stops on **Christmas Day** (including transport), but most establishments treat other public holidays (known in England as bank holidays) the same as Sundays.

Time

During the winter Britain is on **Greenwich Mean Time** (GMT), and in summer (from March to October) on **British Summer Time** (BST), which is one hour ahead of GMT.
Europe: GMT plus 1 hour.
USA, Canada (East): GMT minus 5 hours.
USA, Canada (West): GMT minus 8 hours.
Australia: GMT plus 8–10 hours.
New Zealand: GMT plus 12 hours.
South Africa: GMT plus 2 hours.

Communications

Post: Post offices are generally open ⊕ 09:00–17:30, Mon–Fri; 09:00–12:30 or 13:00, Sat. The Trafalgar Square Post Office (✉ 24–28 William IV St) is open ⊕ 08:00–20:00, Mon–Thu; 08:30–20:00 Fri, 09:00–20:00 Sat.

Postage stamps can be bought at post office counters, from vending machines, and also in many newsagents.

Telephones: Public **payphones** are operated by British Telecom (BT) and most accept coins, credit cards and phonecards.

Phonecards are available from post offices and newsagents and come in denominations of £3, £5, £10 and £20. A few payphones offer Internet access.

London's area code is '020', followed by 8 digits. If you have old listings, use '020-7' in place of '0171' and '020-8' in place of '0181'. When calling within London, you need only the 8-digit number.

Any number beginning '09' is premium rate (can be over £1 a minute) and numbers beginning '07' are mobiles (expensive).

'0800' and '0808' are free lines. Try not to use the phone in your **hotel** room: mark-ups are among the world's highest and it will cost you a lot of money. To make an international telephone call, dial 00, followed by the country code and then the area code:

Australia 61
USA & Canada 1
Ireland 353
New Zealand 64
France 33
Singapore 65
Hong Kong 852
South Africa 27

Operator assistance
☎ 100
International
Operator ☎ 155
Directory assistance
☎ 118 500 or 118 118
International directory assistance ☎ 118 505

Electricity

The current in England is 240 volts AC (50 Hz). Most American or European appliances will need an adaptor – ask your hotel if they can lend you one, otherwise buy one at a chemist (pharmacist) or an electrical shop.

Weights and Measures

The imperial system of measurements has officially been replaced by the metric system, and that is used in shops, etc. (sometimes in tandem with imperial), but imperial is still common in speech.

Health Precautions

No special health precautions are necessary. Most European countries (as well as some Commonwealth countries) have reciprocal health arrangements should you need treatment at an NHS (National Health Service) hospital; you will need to obtain the relevant forms before you leave home. For other nationalities, accident and emergency care is generally free at NHS hospitals' casualty departments, but there'll be a charge for other medical treatment (including hospitalization). It's therefore advisable to arrange comprehensive travel insurance before you leave home.

Personal Safety

Compared to many cities, London is a relatively safe destination and the greatest risk is from thieves and pickpockets hanging around busy shopping streets or on crowded underground platforms or trains. Use common sense and be watchful.

• Don't carry more cash than you will need for the day.
• Keep your wallet or purse out of sight; keep handbags fastened and don't carry a wallet in your back pocket.
• Never leave a handbag, suitcase, or coat unattended.
• Avoid poorly lit, quiet areas (such as parks) after dark. If you are subject to a mugging or robbery,

report it to the local police station (*see* under 'Police' in the phone book, or call Directory Enquiries.

Emergencies

The familiar image of the British 'bobby' plodding the streets endures, although patrol cars now dominate. The police are generally approachable and helpful should you be lost or in trouble. In an emergency for police, fire, ambulance or coastguard dial ☎ 999 or 112.

Disabled Access

Contact Transport for London Access & Mobility, ✉ Windsor House, 50 Victoria St, London SW1H 0TL, ☎ (020) 7222 1234, ⏰ 09:00–17:00, Mon–Fri; 🖥 www.tfl.gov.uk

Etiquette

London tends to be an easy-going place with very few formal dress codes or similar restrictions. A night at the opera or in a really top-class restaurant will, of course, necessitate more formal wear, but otherwise smart, casual clothes will do almost everywhere. The British are inveterate believers in **queueing**, whether it be at a bus stop, in shops or elsewhere, and they don't take kindly to those not prepared to stand in line for their turn. The exception is during the rush hour on tubes, buses and trains, when a free-for-all is more likely to prevail. On the Underground you stand on the right on escalators, and keep the left clear. In recent years **smoking** has become less acceptable in public places and is now totally banned on all **public transport** and also in most public buildings. Restaurants and some hotels are now also increasingly anti-smoking: check before booking your table or room.

Festivals and Events

Late Jan/early Feb • Chinese New Year
March • Ideal Home Exhibition; Chelsea Antiques Fair
Late March/early April • Oxford versus Cambridge Boat Race
April • Flora London Marathon
May • Chelsea Flower Show; Royal Windsor Horse Show
June • Trooping the Colour; Royal Academy Summer Exhibition (runs till Aug); Derby Day and Royal Ascot; Biggin Hill Air Fair
Late June/early July • Henley Regatta; Wimbledon Lawn Tennis Championships
July • Farnborough Air Display; Kenwood Lakeside Concerts (run till Aug); City of London Festival; Henry Wood Promenade Concerts (run till Sept)
August • Great British Beer Festival, Notting Hill Carnival
September • Chelsea Antiques Fair
Late Sept/early Oct • Horse of the Year Show; Costermongers Harvest Festival
November • Lord Mayor's Show; London to Brighton Veteran Car Rally; Guy Fawkes Night; State Opening of Parliament; Festival of Remembrance
December • International Showjumping.

For a full rundown, get the monthly *London Planner* (a free booklet from TICs), or consult *Time Out, What's On* or the *Evening Standard*.

INDEX OF SIGHTS

GENERAL INDEX

GENERAL INDEX

GENERAL INDEX